IF JESUS WAS A RAPPER

CELLUS HAMILTON

To request permissions, contact the publisher at hello@sowandtell.co

Paperback: 9798487257024

Library of Congress Number: 1-10878764901

First paperback edition October 2020.
Edited by Clara Abigail & Hannah Giles
Cover art by Alehandro Petrovic
Layout by Melvyn Paulino
Photographs by Michaelle Chapoteau

Printed by Amazon in the USA.

Sow and Tell LLC
42 Tiemann Place
Suite 418
New York, NY 10027

CellusHamilton.com

ALBUM DISCOGRAPHY

as M.P.H. (Man Praisin Hard)

Life 101, 14 Years Strong (2008)

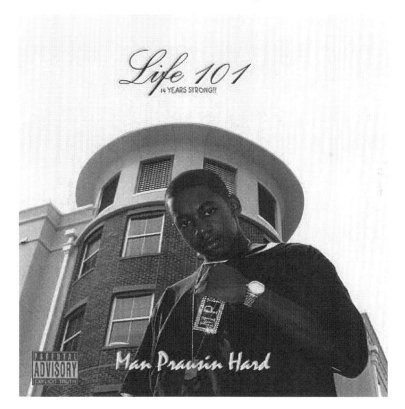

Universal Disturbance (2009)

ALBUM DISCOGRAPHY

as Cellus Hamilton

The Most Beautiful (2014)

We Are & We Shall (2017)

Washing Her Feet (2019)

??? (2022)

CellusHamilton.com

To my family, friends, and the many rappers that raised me. To the black church. To Atlanta.

Dear Reader,

It is a major milestone for me to present this work to you. I began writing this book many years ago in a season where I was not yet mature enough to comprehend the weight of my message. I also did not yet have the authority or experience to speak what was bubbling in my heart. Fast forward to today and I know that you reading this book is the faithful work of the Lord. I've always known I would write a book someday and that it would help inspire a generation of creatives to love and serve God faithfully. I believe this book contains the potential to do just that.

I feel led to write this book because of the 21 years of experience I have in the music industry and ministry. I am a Jesus follower, husband, father, hip-hop artist, business owner, and evangelist. I spend my days mentoring young men, recording music, and developing creatives. I believe this book will shift the priorities of Christian creatives, help them see Jesus more clearly, and remind them to build deep roots in their communities. Internet fame will come and go. Only what we do for Christ will last and there is no societal impact without real-life investment.

Table of Contents

Introduction..15

CHAPTER 1 Bethlehem..17

CHAPTER 2 Nazareth...29

CHAPTER 3 Parables...41

CHAPTER 4 In the Temple...55

CHAPTER 5 Walking on Water...71

CHAPTER 6 Religion Vs Relationship..................................83

CHAPTER 7 Signs & Wonders...97

CHAPTER 8 She's Not My Type...111

CHAPTER 9 Foundations of a Life Together.......................121

CHAPTER 10 To Be Remembered.......................................133

CHAPTER 11 Real Life > Social Media................................143

CHAPTER 12 Sow and Tell...157

CHAPTER 13 Legacy...171

About the Author...181

INTRODUCTION

This book is in no way designed to present me as Jesus or even as a Jesus figure for that matter. Instead, my mission is to change and challenge culture and our view of hip-hop artists in the Christian context. A vast chasm plagues and disrupts how the church values and sees the hip-hop musician and must be destroyed. Though I am still young and have much to live and accomplish within the hip-hop space, I believe that my life experiences and journey as a hip-hop artist have provided great insight into how I view the church and how I love my neighbor. I've had many opportunities to grow and live my life as an expression of the hands and feet of Jesus during these 20 years of performing, writing music, and professionally navigating the music industry. The format of this book will use my life story to draw parallels that may help you see Jesus more authentically and powerfully. I pray that this book will challenge you and help you love and follow our Savior more than ever.

CHAPTER 1

BETHLEHEM

T he two times my feet struggled to move forward are the most significant and life-changing moments of my life. The first moment when I was five years old, listening to the words of Pastor Green give an altar call. In a small church called Mount Zion AME on the north side of Atlanta, I was frozen in place as the opportunity for salvation was being offered. The other moment was the day I proposed to my wife. In both moments, I was entering into a covenant. I was entering into relationships that would forever change the way that I maneuvered through life. Looking back, I'm incredibly grateful to know that these were the only moments I have ever forgotten how to walk. As my legs seemed nailed to the floor, I'm confident that I've counted the cost of the steps I eventually took. And because of these steps, the Lord has graciously allowed me to influence the walk of many others.

Music has always been a part of my life. I grew up in a musical family. My mom was a rapper, and my dad sang in the men's choir. My grandpa played guitar on the radio, and my siblings and I grew up singing in the children's choir at church. We weren't a part of ordinary children's choirs. Instead, we were like young superstars on tour. If you grew up in a black church in Atlanta, you might already know what I'm talking about. AME Churches in Georgia went hard for their children's choirs. Imagine 30 kids squeezing into church vans to drive to the next revival service. I can still remember how amazing it felt singing to God in those purple and gold robes.

Life at home was full of music too. My favorite memories are Saturday mornings as the entire family cleaned the house while my mom played music from the entertainment center. I'm still convinced that music makes you clean better. Some nights it was my mom cooking while music was playing throughout the house. Other times, it was my parents in the living room steppin'. Sometimes, we were all gathered around the tv with the volume muted as we had the music playing. And then there were the times where my family sat listening to me on the speakers. Whatever day you happened to visit the Hamilton home, music was usually our permanent guest.

I released my first album at eleven years old, but I began making music at the age of eight. My mom started taking me to the studio at a young age, and my parents were always driving me to perform all over Atlanta. It was a beautiful era of listening to V103 announce a new talent competition while we leaned in close to the radio to figure out where I'd be performing next. Atlanta is in the Bible belt, meaning that it was a city that supported its youth most strongly. No matter what part of town I was in, I always received love when they learned that I was a gospel rapper. It's just how you were raised, being from there. Even if you didn't go to church, you played gospel on Sundays and appreciated seeing people talk about Jesus.

Being from Atlanta may be the reason why I always felt supported. Nobody ever boo'd the gospel rapper. They may not sing along, but they always gave respect, and at that time, that was enough for me.

Being a child artist, bouncing around from one music showcase to the next, you start to know people and build a network in your city. It was common to see other kid artists and remember each other's songs to sing along whenever one was on the stage. But even from a young age, I always stood out. In school, I was always a great writer and had won many small poetry competitions. I tended to think deeper than other kids. I loved to read. In second grade, I took an AR Test. "AR" stood for accelerated reader, and it tested your reading skills and comprehension. This test revealed that I read on a college level while I was in the second grade. Twelfth-grade, ninth month to be exact!

As people learned about my career and frequent performances on the weekends, older kids gravitated toward me. So many teenagers around me aspired to make music on the same level that they saw me doing it. They were inspired that I was an eleven-year-old with an album in stores and wished their parents would support their dreams the way mine did. I didn't realize this at the time, but this was why teenagers accepted me and allowed me to hang with them and their friends. Many of the older teens from my church would stand in the parking lot, freestyling every week. I was the only kid they allowed in the cypher. This is where I learned how to freestyle, beatbox, and battle rap.

To this day, I'm eternally grateful for those teenagers that accepted me even though I was young. I'm especially appreciative of the teenagers at my church. Though they usually rapped about other things when they were outside of the church parking lot, they were the first ones to show me that you could rap and love Jesus. I thought they were cool and borrowed something from every single one of them. Even though some of them no longer follow Jesus, they are a big reason I'm here today.

Being born in Kansas City, I always felt misrepresented. When people heard Kansas, they always thought of farmland. There weren't many famous black people from there, so many people were left to assume that it was a town full of country white people. That's true, but it's also just like many other cities in the Midwest. Deeply segregated, marginalized, and full of crime.

I moved to Atlanta at five years old and always felt a strong sense of pride being from the Midwest. I didn't speak with a country accent, and I wore big coats in the wintertime. I liked being different from all the other kids, and they liked me because I was different. For example, instead of saying "soda," I said "pop," and instead of saying "the movies," I said "the show." It also meant that my influences were a little different than everyone around me.

My family is from Chicago, and their culture has always been a part of me. It was home before I ever arrived. Growing up in my family, I quickly learned that being from Chicago was the ultimate bragging right. Just the phrase alone meant so many different things all at once. For example, my mom could say "I'm from Chicago," and it would mean "I will fight you," "Who do you think you're talking to?", "I'll be fine," or "I know what I'm doing." I would hear about being in Chicago as a baby and wish that I could remember it. It was deep.

I'm blessed to have grown up having both parents present in the home. But rap music and media culture convinced me that I wasn't blessed. It made me feel like I was less cool because I had both. Like I had to be something I wasn't. Like I had to act like I wasn't loved and cared for like the other kids. I used to think the kids whose parents didn't set curfews had the best life. I used to want to be one of the kids whose parents never called their phones telling them to come home. I thank God that He didn't honor my foolish prayers.

I wasted many years acting like my friends who didn't have fathers at home. I'll never forget seeing my dad in tears when He found out I was smoking weed. It was one of the few moments I had ever seen my dad cry. There was deep sadness and anger in those tears. He wiped his face as he said, "You're out here acting like you don't have a dad who loves you at home. These are things that I did, but you don't have to do these things. You know better."

In my teenage years, I took a few turns that I knew weren't right for me. I was never a bad kid, and I was never even rebellious. But I think that is the very problem. Because I knew God at a young age, I never was able to sin in peace. I always would hear God talking to me while my other friends were numb and felt no conviction for their actions. Imagine living your whole life knowing you've been chosen to represent God but still trying to fit in with the crowd. It's a highly annoying way to live. I hated it. Every time I would curse, people would laugh and say, "you don't say it right. Just stop."

Imagine smoking with your friends, and they always put a limit on how many blunts you can smoke because they say, "Nah, man, you shouldn't be high like us." I remember taking pictures with guns in my hands, and my friends wouldn't snap the photos.

I was a marked man everywhere I went. It was like my friends wouldn't listen to God for themselves, but they would always listen to God about me. At the same time, the streets always held a place for me. People were quick to tell me that I didn't belong there, yet they always welcomed and embraced me. They wouldn't admit it openly, but they secretly felt safer with me around. They felt God's love in having me nearby.

I have worked at every mall in metro Atlanta. And yes! That is no lie or exaggeration. I spent ten years working for Finish Line and another three years working at Lids (Hat World). So retail has been an entire third of my life up to this point. I mention this important part of my story because it has significantly contributed to who I am today. My early work career taught me to serve others and sacrifice even when I didn't feel like it. It's where I learned how people perceived me as a black man and how to relate to people of different cultures. In retail, you serve people from all different backgrounds and deal with an entire world of personalities. Yet, despite all of this, my responsibility every day was to serve the customer. And that's precisely what I did.

My first official job was as a telemarketer in 2007, but that was not my first job. I've been a hustler since birth. During my middle school years, my dad was a barber and owned a barbershop. When school would let out for the day, I would walk to my dad's barbershop to earn some money after school. I would sweep up the hair, take out the trash, and manage the client lists at the front of the shop. Because it was my dad's business, he ultimately was the only one responsible for paying me. But as time went on, the other barbers started paying me once they noticed how well I was keeping their stations cleaned.

I spent a lot of time in the barbershop. And the barbershop is about as hip-hop as it gets. It was the bonding time for me to hang with my dad while he was at work, but it also was where I perceived the many kinds of men who came for a haircut. It was where I learned and observed how my dad acted around other men. It was where I learned remarkable things about the world. You had your dope dealers who came in with the fresh gear and big amounts of cash in rubber bands. You had the hustlers who came in selling polo shirts, air force ones, CDs, and DVDs. (I had a few fake shoes more than a few times). You had the men who came in regularly with their sons for haircuts. You also had the mothers that saw the barbershop as daycare. They would drop their kids off, hoping there was a long wait, so they could run errands and get things done. Then you had the moms that would wait for their sons to get their haircuts.

As life unfolded before me, I was learning and soaking in everything. I was seeing the effect of broken families as it even pertains to getting a haircut. Still, nobody can tell me that the barbershop isn't an important bonding time for father and son. It's just a fact.

The music in the barbershop was always diverse. My dad was a Christian man and was running a barbershop that felt different than the rest. He played gospel—Kirk Franklin, Fred Hammond, and all the mass choirs. He played hip-hop. He played reggae. He played R&B. He even played the CDs from the local rappers who came in. But more than anything, he always played my music. It was beautiful.

Imagine being 11 years old, sweeping up hair in the barbershop, having a steady flow of cash in your pocket, and hearing the music you created in your bedroom blasting on the speakers. These were foundational moments. Another thing that was powerful for me was seeing how many men looked up to my dad. He viewed being a barber as much more than just cutting hair. For him, it was about mentorship, vision casting, and legacy building. He would always tell me, "People can get a haircut anywhere, but they come to me because they know they are going to get more than a haircut."

Most barbershops were places where parents would drop their kids off and pick them up after they had been corrupted by a bunch of degrading conversations about women and loud music with cursing. But my dad ran his shop differently. The barbers and clients respected the culture my dad was building, and they partnered with him to carry out the vision. Anybody who wasn't onboard was fired. I didn't even know it at the time, but my dad was modeling for me how to live a life of integrity where God influenced everything you did.

Eventually, I stopped working at the shop as much. Instead, I started hanging with my friends a little more. And then got caught up wanting a "real job" like the rest of my friends. In hindsight, no future job ever paid me or treated me as well as those middle school years working for my dad.

My mom being a rapper is a huge part of my journey as an artist. Aside from her career, though, my mom is a dynamic mother, which is why I am here today. When I reflect on her, I recognize that she is the embodiment of strength. She is a strong black woman who sacrificed everything so that her family could be successful. She had four kids and was deeply involved in each of our lives. She could give us each a special kind of attention while simultaneously making us feel part of the whole. Her amount of unselfishness still amazes me. I have a permanent image in my head of my mom craving chocolate, buying a snickers bar, yet only taking a small piece while giving the rest to me. This was her life.

My mom made sure that all my siblings and I knew that we were kings and queens. She was quick to correct anyone who spoke a harmful word against her children—even family. That's where I get it from. Some of my most vivid memories are of my mom being my defender. She was quick to pay any of my teachers a visit when they spoke ill of her children. She did this while not being disillusioned with the truth of her children's role in classroom conflicts. As a rapper, words were critical to her. The weight they carried was immense. And she chose her use of them carefully. My mom knew the difference between conviction and condemnation.

She believed that there was no such thing as a bad child. Just children that weren't taught about who they were. And that was how she moved. In my entire life, I've never been called "bad," "lazy," "stupid," or the "n-word" by mom. Because of her example, anyone else calling me anything outside of my name will forever be unacceptable.

Growing up, we always knew that our mom was cool. Whenever we'd be trying to learn a new dance, she already knew how to do it perfectly. She taught us how to think on our feet, roast, and crack jokes on people. She made sure we did our homework and were at school every single day. I had perfect attendance my entire life! She read books to us and set aside time for us to read every single day. She gave us a limit to how long we could play video games and instead encouraged us to be active and play outdoors with kids in the neighborhood. She made sure we kept God first and never missed a Sunday at church. But most importantly, she prayed with us.

I don't write these things to brag but to commission and encourage anyone reading this book that you too can live this way. My mom is a real-life superhero, and the crazy thing is she didn't even know that what she was doing was right. She was just a mom committed to following the Holy Spirit and making sure her kids knew Jesus for themselves.

The same way that I wasn't grateful for my dad until I got older and living on my own was the same way that it was for my mom and me. Life with a praying mother was extremely annoying for me as a teenager. The Lord was always snitching on me.

Every time I was about to have sex, get high, or was somewhere trying to be tough, my mom would always call my phone. She always knew when I wasn't living like the child of God she was raising me to be. Even being a kid from the suburbs, I still remember the two parties where my mom called me to come home early. Both parties were shut down right after I left. One because of a shooting, and the other because of a massive brawl with brass knuckles. My praying mom would get a hunch in her spirit and call me, saying I needed to get home. I'd be mad, but when she'd say, "your dad is on his way," there was nothing more I could do.

These days I'm incredibly grateful that my mom has always been a woman of prayer. Society often talks about how men are affected by dysfunctional fathers but rarely speaks of the mother's role. I've realized that many men struggle in their marriages due to the kind of mothers they had. Men without relationships with their mothers often have a hard time trusting women and allowing themselves to be loved by them. They usually recognize their deep desire to be loved by a woman yet sabotage any loving relationship that attempts to do so. They often won't admit it, but they are afraid of being hurt by a woman again. The pain from their mother's absence cuts too deep.

Black moms naturally defend their children, mainly because America has failed to do so. My mom believed it was not the school's job to feed us. She made sure that she or my dad prepared breakfast for us every morning before we went out into the cold world. It didn't matter that there was food at school. She was going to see to it that we ate something, even if it wasn't much.

Being from Chicago, she didn't want us to "dress country" like everybody else in Georgia. Basketball shorts were for the court, not the classroom. White tees were underwear, not your main shirt. And my Uncle Richard and Auntie Angel always kept us fly with the newest clothes.

My mom taught me to speak my mind. She always said that the knowledge God gave me was powerful and that she believed I was the next Tupac. The world would be offended by the way I used my mind. Still to this day, I often get people who praise my honesty. They desire to speak as honestly as I do and for the courage to go against what's comfortable.

I began working as a telemarketer in 2007. This was probably the most non-hip-hop moment of my life. I was working in a call center and had a cubicle. The job was straightforward. Memorize a script, call a long list of numbers, and don't take "NO" for an answer. Piece of cake. I was 15 years old and had my first real job. While I'm grateful for what I learned while working there, God was very intentional with cutting my time short. This job was in a small hick-town, and I was the only black person there. I also was the youngest, and all my coworkers were inmates working on work release. Nevertheless, I formed some deep friendships at this job and learned some important lessons about people. I've had a soft spot for people in jail ever since.

My career in retail began a year later, in 2008. I started as a sales associate at Finish Line, which did a lot more work than current sales associates do. My very first day was filled with high expectations and low realities, but I appreciated every moment. I was making $5.85 per hour (which was the Georgia minimum wage back in 2008). My boss was a cool black lady from Brooklyn, and I automatically felt safe with her. She handed me a stack of "Winner Circle" pamphlets and told me to stand by the door and greet every customer that entered the store. I was the best greeter she ever hired.

As a Christian, I always made sure to be different than every other worker. I knew I was working for God and wanted people to see Him through me. I worked with integrity and made sure that I was always the top salesman. I went out of my way to serve customers and even stayed later to care for their needs. I cleaned the bathroom. I'd go home exhausted every day, yet confident that the Lord was proud of me. I always knew that one day I wouldn't have to work so hard.

Many times, I was offered job promotions to become a manager, but I consistently refused. I was in school, playing sports, and maintaining my professional music career on the side. I knew I didn't have the time for a full-time job. During this time, I was consistently the top sales associate in the State of Georgia and would frequently travel to other stores to pick up shifts and make some extra money whenever I could. After doing this for a while, I quickly grew tired of driving many miles to work at other malls and accepted a position in management. I can't tell you how many managers and employees got fired for stealing, but just know that they always defended my name as a man of integrity even on their days of being escorted out by police.

For many years, I felt like I was wasting my life. I would work 12-hour shifts, standing all day, doing physical labor, and dealing with customers. Smiling was a part of the job, and I did it even when I was exhausted.

Then, soon as I left work, I was back to mugging again. I sometimes napped in the food court between conference calls. And somewhere between this time, I bounced between several positions and companies. Assistant manager at Finish Line, Manager at Macy's, Assistant manager at Lids, to Store Manager at Lids. I felt like I lived in the mall, and I'd often be at a different mall every day of the week.

I saved a lot of gas money by taking the Marta, Gwinnett County bus, and the Cobb County buses. I would use the bus to catch up on my sleep and avoid nodding off in Atlanta traffic. I worked so much; I didn't have any time for myself. I wasn't spending any money, and I wasn't even working on music. I was drowning in work and saw no end in sight.

The natural flow of this book will resemble the journey that you've begun to experience so far. A beautiful blend of the church, family, music, and the black experience awaits you. All these pieces of my life have been intentionally woven together by God and play a huge role in my journey to maximize my impact for Christ. Believing in Jesus and what He did for me has been a huge part of my life for as long as I can remember.

Despite all the changes and rollercoasters in my life, hip-hop has remained constant. It has also been the tool that has helped me know and experience God more than anything else in my life. In fact, along with seeing Jesus as God, Master, and many other sacred things, I've also identified Jesus as being my favorite rapper. My hip-hop lifestyle has given me a unique bend and imagination that is always present when I read the Bible. And it has transformed the way that I exist in the world. I hope you'll accept my invitation to a deeper exploration of where these two worlds meet.

CHAPTER 2

NAZARETH

At the beginning of my career, I went by the name "MPH" (Man
Praisin' Hard). It was a rap name given to me by my dad. "MPH"
are the initials to my full name which is, Marcellus Preston
Hamilton. Man Praisin' Hard was who I was. Although my overall artist
DNA was the same then as it is now, I was not yet walking in the fullness
of who God had created me to be. Much of the passion you have come to
recognize from me today was still there. However, I was arrogant, cocky,
and immature. I served God from a place of entitlement and pride, often
believing that I was solely the answer to the music industry's problems.
While I never want to give the impression that I've arrived, I do want to
make it very clear that I have come a long way.

My earliest music and albums are still online, as I've left them there
for your enjoyment and listening pleasure. One of the amazing things
that I always notice when listening to my old music is how clear my
understanding of the Gospel is. Every song oozed the message of Jesus
Christ's death on the cross, his resurrection, and the new life that we
have in Him. My flow was solid, my voice was commanding, and my
heart was pure. You could tell that this child had a deep understanding
and love for the Bible. But off stage, I was a mess.

Still to this day, my heart cringes when I think of the many relationships that Man Praisin' Hard rubbed the wrong way. I was the kind of artist who talked bad about other artists behind their back, particularly artists I had never met. I was caught up in crazy conspiracy theories that believed a Christian couldn't succeed without making a bargain with Satan. I lacked hope, depth, and experience. Yes, it's true! I was a flashy artist with an ugly inside. But Jesus and many years of experience have shaped me into the man I am today. And finally, I have come to the place of being grateful for my past and the many mistakes I've made. Beautiful people do not just happen. They are shaped by life's failures and falls.

And for this reason, many of my critiques toward artists today are not theologically based; but are instead based on my experiences. Character is built over time—through maneuvering challenging and career-threatening situations. Experience will teach you to lean on God and will often correct the many thoughts and wrong assumptions that we hold deep inside.

Man Praisin' Hard was known all around Atlanta. Or at least his arrogance made him believe he was. I'll never forget the night I had a performance at Apache Café. Apache Cafe was a frequent popular spot for me to perform at least once a month, as they were always having some of the best showcases and industry execs from all over the world present to scout new artists. Because of this, it was also the number one place for an artist to get scammed. Here I was, with all my friends, having signed up for one of the biggest nights of my life—to perform for major industry execs from Def jam, Atlantic records, and many other prominent labels. Artists were driving from all over the country to be a part of the showcase that night. Many artists were not guaranteed to perform but decided to go the many miles to Atlanta to test their chances anyway. I had been blessed with an email confirmation securing my performance slot for the night, and I was ready.

As the evening was underway, I stood there in the crowd for two hours as countless artists performed on stage, giving it their best shot. I had already checked in with the stage manager twice at this point, who could only tell me, "Your slot is coming up soon." As the evening dragged on, more and more of my friends that I came with began to leave, acknowledging that they had been there too long. They wished they could stay and support me but had other things to do the next day. In a desperate effort to not lose the crowd, I once again approached the stage manager respectfully, asking when I was slated to perform. This time I noticed a group of artists walking in the door that I hadn't seen before. As I overheard them explaining how far they had driven to be there, I witnessed an artist slide a handful of cash to the stage manager. The stage manager immediately responded by telling him that he would be performing next. I couldn't believe what I was seeing. It was not that I wasn't able to believe that this was how the industry worked, but that I had been so naïve not to understand why I hadn't performed yet.

At that moment, I decided that if other people would break the rules, I would also break the rules. So I returned to my friend Jeff who was waiting for a response about when I would be performing. I told him I was next.

During the next break, when the stage manager got on stage to announce the next artist, I rushed onto the stage. I snatched the mic out of his hand and demanded the DJ to play my music. As the host reached to get the mic back from me, I began to bash him in front of the crowd. I put the whole club on notice about how bogus the stage manager was and continued to demand the DJ to play my music. When the DJ played my music, I went crazy on stage. To this day, it had to be one of the angriest and aggressive performances I've ever seen. All the energy was there, but of course, because my heart wasn't right, everything that I was saying was not felt by the audience. After my performance, I left the stage angrily, gathered my friends, and left the venue. We were upset because none of the industry execs that we planned to perform in front of were even there when I had performed.

This is just one of the many examples highlighting the way that Man Praisin' Hard handled situations. I also damaged the integrity of my character and career through many other means. I had raw talent at this stage but did not know how to steward it properly. I believed deeply that I was the best rapper in the world, and that was my biggest problem.

Every attempt to "network" in those days was an attempt to prove that I was better than the person who already accomplished more than me. I often went to concerts to get backstage to prove that I was better than the headlining artist. My empty compliments and pitiful request for a mentor were often recognized as immediate disguises for my arrogance. While I still believe I was working harder than many of those artists I was envious of, my ego and heart posture prevented me from being a vessel that the Lord could use. He needed me to be completely humbled, completely broken, and completely dependent on Him for my success.

Much of this humility only came throughout the years, as I was consistently humiliated from my failure and mistakes. Humiliation and humility derive from the same word. The Lord needed me to stop leaning on my musical talent and to become so dependent on His leading so that I would be fully surrendered for Him to use. Much of that lesson came through college.

In 2010, I graduated from high school and entered my freshman year of college at Howard University. Being at Howard University was my first time living away from home and my first step toward independence. I had always known that I would attend an HBCU and was excited to be in that number of successful black men. During my high school years, I took summer classes at Morehouse College in Atlanta. My parents always assured me that college was an amazing opportunity for you to experience a new city while still having a basic sense of security.

Being a city boy and not knowing much about DC made Howard seem like the perfect choice. I'm extremely grateful that the Lord landed me at Howard University, and much of my life and the success that I've acquired is owed to my college years. These were the years where I was challenged the most. For the first time in my life, I was living outside of the Bible belt. Though I was amongst a community of people that looked like me, there was a diverse spectrum of religious and spiritual belief systems. Not everyone was a Christian, and even the Christian people demonstrated the diversity of black Christianity.

Not only did I receive a top-tier education from Howard University, but I also received a top-tier education about my history as a black man in America. Original manuscripts, books, and resources exclusive to Howard's campus filled our library. They were historical documents here that existed nowhere else in the world, and I had access to all of them. Even my most introductory courses, such as freshman seminar, were way more extensive than any public school's black history course. This is communicated even in the context of telling you about the kind of home that I grew up in. As a child, both of my parents would sit my siblings and me down regularly to watch films, documentaries and even read books about black history. I remember Martin Luther King Day not as a holiday from school but as a day where my parents would have us write papers and essays about black history. One of my dad's famous sayings was "..., but they won't teach you that in school."

I bring up my foundation because this is generally everyone's story as they enter an HBCU. We entered college as those who had deep frameworks about our history and a fierce love for our beautiful skin. But, we would all go on to learn how much more still lie uncovered.

This level of awakening, which I believe can only take place on an HBCU campus, is both beautiful and spiritual. To have your college campus become the central point where all facets of the African Diaspora meet and converge is a miracle. In college, I discovered Africans who spoke Spanish, French, Italian, and other languages that we often deem to be associated with a white European face. It was there that I learned about the racism that existed within my people.

Even the ways we segregated ourselves on campus as if we were not all from the same place. College was also the place where my faith was strengthened the most. There were generally two camps. One camp believed in Jesus and was deeply convinced more than ever that He was God in the flesh. The other camp aggressively rejected Jesus and anything that had to do with him. This camp was deeply scarred by the generations of abuse inflicted upon black bodies by white people who claimed to adhere to the very Gospel they used to justify their atrocities. It was in this world where I began to wrestle with my questions about Jesus, and I'm incredibly grateful for this wrestle to this day. I firmly believe that a faith that has never been tested is no faith at all. As my daily conversations and environment drove me to read books about the history of Christianity, I began to realize that America was nowhere near the birth of Christianity. That Christianity's roots were deeply African and Middle Eastern and that even our most prized theologians had been whitewashed and stripped from their real ethnic origins.

It was this journey and these questions that reignited my faith like never before. Jesus was no longer someone that I trusted simply because of my parents and family. He was now my God because I had wrestled with Him, just like Jacob.

I do believe that it's important to note that there was never a day in my life where I ultimately questioned Jesus as Lord. I had grown up in the church and had always known Jesus intimately and personally since I was a child. His voice was familiar to me, and I knew He was real. My college questions were never an indictment on His validity but rather how His sovereignty coexisted with my black identity. This confidence that I held about Jesus is owed solely to my healthy church experiences and my family practicing what they preached in public at home. These questions in this season of my life were pivotal in helping me dig deeper into my faith. It was also crucial in my development as an artist and as a man of God. Because of my journey at Howard University, I can now stand in front of any man, with any amount of knowledge or any claim, unafraid of what he may say—rooted in the fact that I personally and deeply know Jesus.

College was a time that transformed my music more than any other. I was an Atlanta kid from the Midwest who was now attending an HBCU in DC. DC was known as Chocolate City. A hub for some of the wealthiest black people in America, many of whom served in significant political and government roles. Go-Go music, which I've never been fond of, was the soundscape. Beats and lyricism merged here. Black excellence was in the air. Black consciousness was in the soil. I pulled from all of these.

When I arrived in DC and checked into my Dorm at Drew Hall, my unspoken goal was to take over my new city. I was so used to performing and being known all over Atlanta that a small city like DC seemed like it would be easy to conquer. I had been selling CDs out of the trunk of my car in Kroger parking lots for years. I had mixtape clientele in every barbershop on Cobb Parkway. So I knew making a mark in a city that was only 68 square miles would be a piece of cake.

I always felt it was cooler not to be from the place where I currently lived. When I was living in Atlanta, everybody associated me with Kansas City & Chicago. When I moved to DC, everybody associated me with Atlanta. People appreciate you more when you're a guest. Atlanta hip-hop was extremely popular in DC, just like it was everywhere else. We had stolen the crown from NY and showed no signs of relinquishing it. I knew I had that true Atlanta style, and I knew everybody in DC would appreciate what I was bringing to the scene.

When I started performing in DC and at Howard University's campus events, I quickly realized how diverse my audience was. Students from HU came not only from all over America but from all over the globe. I fully realized how my music would need global polishing if I were going to break out in my new home. I had never known that Baltimore had their style of music, I never knew about Jersey, and I was ignorant of the Cali swag. It was here where I learned how to adapt.

My mom always taught me that we are a product of the people we surround ourselves with—that no one person has a monopoly on style. Instead, everyone finds two or three things they love about someone else and adopts them into themselves. This is how style is created. The pool of people that I adopted my style from had been relatively small up to this point. But the expansive campus of Howard University exposed me to a whole world of styles. I also think my college years were formative because, at the age of 17, I was still deciding who I would be. Would I fade into the background and conform to the dominant culture around me, or would I forge a new path based on my new opportunities?

One of the things I adopted into my creative process at Howard was parable writing. Most of the people I was performing for were drunk college students who were emotionally and spiritually wide open. Alcohol made them honest, vulnerable, and willing to share the parts of their lives that were often buried deep when they were sober. This meant that I had an opportunity to create music that made them feel loved instead of abandoned. Forgiven, instead of condemned. But I noticed that they didn't sing along if it sounded like I was preaching. So, I practiced writing party songs with double meanings. I wanted the music to keep the party going while simultaneously feeding their souls.

As I was hustling and competing with the other rappers on campus, I was determined to maintain a steady number of live performances each week. I would perform anywhere I could go on campus. Eventually, I expanded out to performing anywhere with a stage in DC. From there, the entire DMV area. I remember borrowing cars from some of my senior friends and driving 2 hours south deep into Virginia for concerts. During this time, I was extremely busy practicing my newfound style of songwriting. I was learning which types of songs were crowd favorites and building my performance skills. Unfortunately, this was also when I started getting rejected from many churches that felt like my Christian message wasn't clear in my music. Many of them thought that I wasn't preaching the Gospel and refused to support me.

Looking back, I was initially deterred by the lack of support from churches, but this ended up being the best thing for my career. The Lord was using the church's rejection to put me back in front of the people He had equipped me to reach my entire life. I had no other choice but to leave the church concerts behind me and begin performing in the local clubs. Most of the clubs would be full of Howard students, and I always appreciated the challenge of performing in those spaces. Howard crowds are notoriously known for being tough critics and were very quick to tell you if they didn't like you. While many artists would have been discouraged by this, all of this drove me to keep perfecting my craft. To keep sharing the Gospel in a slick way. I was finally becoming myself.

Life experiences are a great teacher if you learn from them. I've done many things I'm not proud of, and there have been many moments that I wish I could redo. There are many things I wish I hadn't said. And in this era, where cancel-culture is at an all-time high, I fully understand how scary this is for any modern-day leader. If Twitter would've existed back when I was a kid artist running around Atlanta, I would've been canceled, and you would never know about me right now. But I believe in extending Grace to people because there will come a day where I need that same Grace.

I used to say I was the most hated Christian rapper. The funny thing is that it wasn't true when I first started declaring it, but I spoke it into existence. The very words that I spoke ended up becoming the reality of my life and career. I noticed that in every room I entered, people disregarded me. Every concert I went to trying to network or meet another artist that I was a fan of ended up being an embarrassing insult of how much the artists didn't want anything to do with me. I would reach out for features and get turned down. It was a horrible reality, yet one that I had fully created.

While the horrors of that phase in my career were many, the Lord, in His kindness, ultimately used it for my good. The rejection of many artists and culturemakers that I admired meant I would have to build my own table and chairs. It meant that I would have to become an entrepreneur and forge my relationships with producers and artists instead of schmoozing off the already established ones.

When I was going by the rap name MPH, I deeply loved Jesus, but I was saturated with pride. I was a terrible listener and felt no one had anything to offer except me. I made sure to brag about myself in every song and to speak about how cool I thought I was. I arrived at shows and concerts unwilling and uninterested in engaging with the other artists on the flyer. I talked crazy to promoters and got violent with DJs. I walked all over my fans and supporters and only focused on the numbers. I believed I was entitled.

Writing these things about my past is embarrassing because I know how powerful first impressions are. I know that many artists and industry people still remember this version of myself very well. I know that there are conflicts in people's minds that are even worse than I remember them. But ultimately, I'm grateful. I'm thankful that Jesus never stopped working to make me into His image. I was arrogant yet connected to Jesus. And because He creates the change, my connection to Him allowed Him to invade my life. When I realized that I was already loved and accepted by God, it showed me that I no longer needed to fight to convince people of my talent. It allowed me to appreciate other artists without feeling like their success equaled my failure. I was able to respect when people said they didn't see the benefit of us working together.

I am fully convinced that everything we are stems from understanding the Gospel and Christ's love for us. When I was in college, I sent my music to a man I admired spiritually. We shared a common taste in music, and my relationship with him personally allowed me to have a deep respect and appreciation for the rebukes and advice he offered me. Then, one day, he listened to my music and told me something I desperately needed to hear. He said, "You are such an amazing rapper that you don't have to shout it as these other artists do. They shout it because, deep down, they don't believe it. Saying it makes them feel like it's true. People can tell you're great because God is with you. So don't ever say it. You don't have to."

From that moment, I remember feeling a deep understanding of God's love come over me. It was an entirely new level of confidence. Finally, I was free from rejection.

I mention my early character struggles and even the faith challenges I went through during college because they were the launching pad to my integrity and success. The areas where we are tested become the areas where we have authority and influence. If I would never have been humiliated in my arrogance, then I would not know the power of resting in God's validation instead of fighting for my own. And having to make music for a hostile crowd of partying college students is where I learned how to create music that was faithful to the Gospel while not condemning my unsaved listeners. Finally, and most notably, my wrestle with the blackness and validity of Jesus trained me to speak powerfully against the deception and lies of a western Christianity that removed dignity from black people. In imagining Jesus as a rapper, I feel comfort in recognizing that His journey involved the same.

Before Jesus began His ministry, He was first tested. But unlike myself, Jesus was perfect and defeated all the temptations placed in front of Him. When He was tempted to use His power to satisfy Himself and to turn the stone to bread, He quoted the Word of God and boldly refused. Because of this moment of obedience, we later see Jesus exercising authority in this same area that once tempted Him. As a result, he provides bread and fish for thousands of people on two different occasions.

Next, the devil takes Jesus to the highest point of the temple and tells Him to jump off, quoting scripture to persuade Him. But Jesus responds with scripture, and once again, boldly refuses. Because Jesus didn't listen to the devil's temptation regarding death, He later exercised His authority over death by dying on the cross at God's appointed time and rising from the grave three days later. Jesus was walking in a level of authority that we can trace back to His days in the wilderness. And finally, when Jesus said "No" to the third temptation, which was to bow down and worship the devil in exchange for a worldly kingdom, He was gaining authority over all the kingdoms of this world, which He later proclaimed and demonstrated.

If Jesus was a rapper, I believe He would use all the trials and struggles of His past as preparation for His future assignment. His struggles would not be hidden but instead would be widely documented, as they prove evidence of the strength of God and not man. I believe He would recognize that the enemy's attacks are always a foreshadowing of how God intends to use a person. He would rap about His struggles and about how God's power kept Him amid the storm.

CHAPTER 3

PARABLES

I have always been passionate about helping people to understand the Bible. When it comes to explaining the Bible or even bringing it up in everyday conversation, my face completely lights up as the energy and passion exude through my being. Ever since I was a child, I've been in love with reading the Bible and have had a deep connection to the words that it says. I've long recognized that many people are blind to the goodness of God because they haven't read the Bible for themselves. Instead, they base their perceptions about God and the truth of His Word on what others have told them.

As I've had first-hand experience of the Lord's love for me, it has made me dive deeper into making sure that His Word is understood in the music that I create and write. I believe I am responsible for dismantling the many misconceptions that culture has about the Bible and what it teaches. My new challenge then becomes less about presenting the Gospel and more about choosing *how* to communicate it. In America, our problem is not that we are ignorant of the Gospel; it is that we have grown too familiar. With this understanding, I sit down and write.

I read the messages of Jesus, and I look closely at the audience that He is speaking to. I notice His attention to detail, and I observe that His method of communication is through stories and parables. I hear His compassion, and I feel His love. And then instantly, I'm transported back into my world. I look outside my window and see sheep without a shepherd. The diversity of worldviews within one block is astounding. In my neighborhood, the teacher is hip-hop. It determines what we say, how we walk, what we believe, and even what we do. My neighbors don't go to church, but they've got a Spotify subscription. So I guess I've got to bring the church to them.

I didn't grow up in the projects. I didn't grow up in a single-parent household. I grew up going to church with two parents who loved my siblings and me and worked hard to provide for us every day.

Before Kanye West broke into the industry, hip-hop and its image were very one-sided. To be a credible rapper, you had to be from the streets. Kanye West entered the rap game as an artist that was raised in a middle-class two-parent household. He was educated. He didn't have the traditional hip-hop hood story, yet he was still hip-hop in how he saw the world.

Kanye West has, hands down, inspired me more than any other creative. He is so expressive and artistic that he rubs people in many ways. All the great creatives do. There are many things I admire about Kanye West. I deeply respect his ability to say what he feels. Nowadays, we seem to value people who are best at filtering their opinions and not offending anyone. We are even trained to correlate a person's mental stability based on them expressing their honest opinion. If you are the most honest person, you will be known as the craziest person. I love how Kanye stands on his views no matter what. Despite how we feel about Kanye, he will continue to create art that pushes boundaries and forces you to think. I believe this is the artist's job.

There are two artists that people always say I remind them of. The first is Lupe Fiasco, and the second is Kendrick Lamar. I feel like if anybody says you sound like Lupe, it is automatically a compliment. I've studied so much of Lupe that it completely makes sense. I think my study of him allows me not to be surprised at the comparison, and it's an honor to be compared to such an amazing artist and lyricist.

Another artist who has had a tremendous impact on me is Canton Jones. In Atlanta, Canton Jones was the gatekeeper of Gospel hip-hop. Though he was originally from Florida, He was a Morehouse alum and embraced the city as his own. He was an amazing performer, and his passion and boldness for God were contagious. He had a way of making worship and surrender seem cool, and his music catalog provided anthems that helped my generation navigate through tough situations. Canton Jones is also one of the only gospel dudes I can remember that had the dope boys and killers at his concerts. Regardless of who tricked them into being there, they were often profoundly impacted, flooding the alter seeking repentance and salvation.

In my house, we were all Canton Jones superfans. We understood the skill in his writing, and we also understood how non-traditional he was in his approach. As a black urban family, we understood what Canton Jones represented. A lot of churches were envious of how much Canton's music resonated with the youth. They couldn't seem to get kids to remain in church during any other time except for during a gospel hip-hop concert.

Still to this day, I recognize how important it is to give honor publicly. Canton Jones' song "Cute" kept me from having sex during my teenage years, and his song "Stay Saved" kept me from getting kicked out of school. I'm confident that I'm not the only one whose life was impacted by his music. Having music that reminds you to live a life pleasing to God is extremely important. The effect that it had on my life deeply inspired me to do the same. I desire to make music that will push people towards a personal relationship with God. I grew up witnessing Canton Jones take over clubs, skating rinks, and malls. I endeavor to do the same thing.

Hip-hop is a worldview. It was birthed similarly to the underground railroad. It was birthed as a means for Black and Latinos to talk about what was going on in the hood without being understood by the white man. The same way that the underground railroad was us communicating how we would escape to freedom in code, hip-hop was a code language. Hip-hop was how we could talk about police brutality and what was going on in the streets. If you were from hip-hop soil and understood the code, you were educated and instructed by the music. If you were an outsider, you'd listen to it, enjoy it on a surface level, but you weren't able to decipher what it was ultimately saying. This is what I mean when I speak about the hip-hop lens.

I connect this back to Kanye because his inclusion in hip-hop was based on him understanding the code. His understanding of the code allowed him to speak the code even though the reality of his culture and upbringing was different than the general narrative. He understood that his story needed to be told even though it was different. He knew the streets would appreciate his story because the streets included people like him. When other artists heard his music, they understood that he spoke their language and embraced him even though his story wasn't the same. This is what I think is so powerful about hip-hop. His excellence with production allowed hip-hop culture to embrace him. This was something we hadn't seen before and is a huge reason why I am here today. It assured me that hip-hop had a place for me. That I could be myself. That the only metric for being accepted in hip-hop was to be excellent.

As a man raised in hip-hop, I consider myself proficient at speaking and understanding the language. I tend to present a hidden message within a music soundscape. And I think this is very similar to what Jesus did while He was on earth. I believe if Jesus were here in America during this time, He would be a rapper. He spoke in parables, and He would often share in-depth stories about the kingdom in a particular way depending on who He was talking to. His presentation and storytelling were different if His audience were shepherds than if He were speaking to sheep. And then, the Bible also tells us that for His disciples, He would talk to them plainly and not using parables. This is hip-hop at its core. To use language to communicate truth in the most digestible way and to discern your audience correctly, so you know how to make sure they hear you—or not hear you. Jesus spoke the code according to His listeners, and He forced them to dig deep to find out what He was saying. As a person who loves Jesus and seeks to be like Him in every way, I've committed to following His example.

My creative process is honest. A lot of times, when I'm writing songs, music, or recording verses, I try to put out the first thing that is in my mind or on my heart. This is beautiful because it is authentic, but it can also be dangerous because it can allow me to speak unprocessed and unfiltered thoughts. I try to create music from an honest place that is completely in tune with how I feel while still being mindful and prayerful in sitting with the record for a while. I ask myself filter questions such as: "Is this faithful to what the Word of God says? How is this going to lead people? Is this going to confuse people?" And it usually results in deep prayer and fasting before I decide to release a song. I have conversations with my wife, friends, accountability partners, and pastors, inviting them to discuss the music and what they think about it. I've had many times where songs that I have released were shelved and were not released. This is the part of my process that the fans never see. The deep prayer and processing of whether my song is in the approval of God or if it is fighting for the fickle opinion of hip-hop heads or church people. Whenever I have affirmed counsel and the confident realization that the Lord will be pleased with me by the song's release, I confidently release the song.

When I was young, I approached songwriting by trying to be as creative as possible and do something that no one had ever done before. One day I realized that this posture was preventing me from being creative. The more that I tried to force creativity and impress people, the more I became regular. Eventually, I learned that my creative process began with a deep questioning of myself. "What makes me? What do I like? What are the things that are unique to my personality?" Once I committed to being a hundred percent myself in the music, I tapped into my true creativity as an artist. That's the way I seek to approach all my art. This method ensures that no matter what style the art is in if I approach it being myself, it will always be great. Approach art by being yourself, being authentic, and allowing the naturally flowing creativity in you.

As my music history has made clear, I am not against collaborating with artists or creatives who don't share my faith. For example, if Drake hit me up right now and said, "Let's collaborate," I would do the same thing that I would do if an artist with zero fans reached out to me. First, I am going to pray and seek the Lord about it. The second thing I will do is listen to the song they ask me to be part of. If the song allows room for me to be who God has genuinely created me to be, and the Lord has given me peace about collaborating, then I will be part of the song. If the music does not allow me to be myself and requires me to change who I am to be part of it, I will refuse the offer. It makes no sense for me to be on a song if I can't be who God has made me. I don't believe the legalistic rule that says Christian artists can't collaborate with non-Christians. When you are so good at being confidently who the Lord has created you to be, other people will make room to accommodate you. The world is attracted and drawn to Christians who are confident in who they are in Christ.

As far as hip-hop competition goes, I don't believe there is an authentic expression of hip-hop without understanding the competitive nature of hip-hop. If I get on a record with you, I'm trying to make people never want to listen to you again. That's my goal. I feel like that's what hip-hop is about. When I pick a feature, it's for two things. It's because I completely respect you and because I want to test you. And this is something that hip-hop heads understand. When that artist accepts the feature, they should realize this. And when I accept verses from people, I have the mindset that this artist just signed up for me to murder them on their own song. It's all love. But this is important to hip-hop culture.

I have a vision board in my room that I look at every day. It is filled with reminders and crucial truths vital to me remaining grounded and on track with everything I am doing. For example, one of the things I have written on there is, "I'm successful because I'm doing what God wants me to do and not what man wants me to do." I must look at that every day because as I continue to follow the Lord, He often leads me to speak things that aren't well-received by the culture.

I've written songs and spearheaded movements that have been greatly opposed, particularly by many churches. One example of this is with my album "Washing Her Feet." I've used language that people have disagreed with, and I feel like I'm the most honest and expressive artist I can be.

For example, when you are in conflict, you don't always use the healthiest words you know you should use. And when I communicated this on my album, many people felt like I had gone too far.

I meet a new rapper every day. And I believe the difference between a rapper and an artist is seen in their ability to adapt to the changing climate. As an artist that has committed himself to the craft, I've worked hard to put myself in a position to ensure that my art is well-rounded— that if people get tired of lyricism and they want something fun, I can provide that. If they want lyricism, I can give them that. I can do both. Sadly, many artists can only do one. But it's important to note that all the legends we admire have shown us that no album sounds the same. They can adjust to whatever the music climate is centered on. As an artist, I can pull on all my inspirations and create whatever I choose. I believe I'm here to stay.

As a dreamer, I try my best to bring the visions and dreams that I have in my head to reality. I always feel like an aspect of myself, and even all of humanity, identifies with the royalty aspect of who we are. I'll be sure to make clear that the only reason I have any claim to royalty is because of my shared bloodline with Christ. I'm a child of the King of Kings. And my faith has made that a literal statement. His blood runs in my veins.

I have recognized that I tend to be rebellious when it comes to the music industry rules. I don't like the feeling that I'm an artist confined by music's conventions. The industry is constantly changing, but at one point, it was all about testing the waters with singles before dropping a full-length album. It's not that I disagree with this being logical and wise. I know the value of seeing how the fans respond to a particular sound or pallet of music before releasing the full project. But, as it usually is in my case, I'm focused on making complete bodies of work, which means that I don't want to spoil any of the stories before it's time.

In the true vein of creativity, I believe an artist should do what's in their heart. This is the only guaranteed way to leave an impact on the industry. All the other moves we make to follow the rules leave us blending in with everyone else.

The most challenging thing about making an album is getting the project done. I usually start with a brainstorming sheet full of concepts, topics, maybe some song titles, and subject matter. My challenge is often realized in making that brainstorming sheet a reality. Telling the story and making sure everything fits. Fighting to stay loose with my creativity while also maintaining faithfulness to the ideas that I've written down is a balancing act.

It isn't a coincidence that my songs detailing my real-life experiences always perform better than songs that communicate about someone else's experience. Songs that talk about what I've personally been through resonate on a much deeper level. There's no doubt about it.

I've never been a huge fan of explaining my music and its meaning to people. The explanation often takes away from the appreciation and personal interpretation of the music. Therefore when people ask me to tell them what the song is about, I usually flip their questions back on them and ask them the same. Whatever they believe the song is about, within reason, of course, is exactly what the song is about. Music is an art and shouldn't have a formula instructing people how to receive it. Artists have often robbed consumers of the spiritual experience of interpreting a much larger message than the artists themselves.

My question when starting a song is always the same. How can I give people this amazing, good news that has saved me but not let them know that I'm giving it to them? My years as an artist have taught me that people don't always like to know what they're getting. We love the process of discovery. This makes my goal to do well at delivering the message while still allowing ample space for the listener to do the work of discovery.

As a Christian artist, everything I do has a common goal—to spread the Gospel of Jesus and let people know that He loves them unconditionally. But many times, my method and approach to sharing this message change. It often depends on the season that I am in. For example, all my albums generally represent particular seasons of my life. They are characterized by sonic patterns, themes, topics, and moods. On certain albums, my approach has been very forward. I am telling the Gospel in every song. Even when I've done this, it was still using parables and symbolic language. I believe the message should never be separate from artistic and creative delivery.

On the other hand, there have been certain albums and seasons where I have not been blatant with my message. Generally, in these seasons, I choose to use the power of questions. I often will create songs that force the listener to wrestle with questions in hopes that they will do so faithfully and honestly. The honest wrestling with the questions in our lives will always lead us back to the cross. This is the beauty of artistic strategy and the outcome of many hours of prayer.

In my album "We Are & We Shall," I tackled the challenge of summarizing the flow of humanity. To me, it can be seen in the tug of war of our affections. Desiring to grab hold of God while failing to let go of the idols we set in His place. This album is highly conceptual, even down to its tracklisting. The very migration of humanity eastward, away from the Garden of Eden, is depicted in the music. Creating art like this is what made me fall in love with hip-hop. Reading this, there is no way you would likely conclude that this album is not overtly Christian. It is. But my favorite thing about this album is the response pattern that I continue to receive from listeners. "Wow! It wasn't until my fourth time listening that I realized this album was about God." And for me, that is an actual reward! This is what hip-hop is supposed to be.

Every time we listen to a new album by Kendrick Lamar, we catch something new that we didn't notice before. It is music that invites us into a journey. It challenges our thought patterns. It gives us the potential to be corrected—to find out that we are wrong about what we believe most.

As I'm writing this, I'm reminded of the importance of balance. As much as music is powerful when it allows the listener to embark on the journey of discovery, this is not music's only purpose. A huge part of music's purpose is for entertainment. Entertainment in its root meaning means "to divert one's attention." I enjoy listening to music, particularly when

I want to silence my mind and not have to think. To be able to simply enjoy the music at face value without exercising my brain and relax. This is why I try very hard to never fall into a one-sided pattern. I fully understand that I'll always have many fans who love my music for its high-level lyricism, but I also must remember hip-hop's roots. Hip-hop was created to remind people of color that they could still party and laugh even though America was trying to destroy their very existence. If you were blessed to make it home after a bogus situation with the police, hip-hop reminded you that you were resilient. This is why I write.

There have been times in my career where I've gone down the rabbit hole of lyricism. In striving to be a lyrical scientist, I alienated the very people I set out to reach in the first place. I had no choice but to find the balance. I think this disconnect is often the demise of many of our favorite emcees. I don't want to sacrifice the listener's enjoyment of the music because I'm so busy trying to offer them something. Making great music is about meeting people where they are and being sensitive to their needs. Sometimes I have no choice but to get on that level. Other times, I can relax a little bit. The Holy Spirit has never let me down in telling me which one is appropriate.

Finding this balance is already not easy. But this makes me extremely grateful to be from Atlanta. One of the most notable things about my city is that we naturally approach music in a fun way. In fact, at one time, we were widely criticized because people said our hip-hop was "too fun." They felt like it lacked depth and seriousness. But honestly, we were reflecting on something that hip-hop had always been. The world had just forgotten and was seeing it in a new way in the hands of a new generation. Atlanta had the whole world trying to compete to make the best dance music. We made "Lean Wit It Rock Wit It," we made "Laffy Taffy," and we made "Shoulder Lean." This, too, is hip-hop. And I thank the Lord that I come from that.

Switching back and forth between making serious music and fun music is second nature to me. As a kid artist traveling around Atlanta, I performed in places where the hosts would be playing the newest dance songs before and after each performer. The crowds were there, ready to gather at the stage and dance. This meant that if you didn't hold the crowd's attention, they would likely start a dance circle in the crowd and completely ignore your performance. This was a natural and real thing from my environment. And as a young, arrogant rapper from Atlanta, I refused to share the spotlight with anyone. I needed all eyes on me.

I value an artist that prioritizes educating the people. Education has always been important to hip-hop. Hip-hop was created to educate. When rappers in the South Bronx started hip-hop, it was to educate about the community we were living in—getting the audience to see the world differently and be more conscious and aware. Not trying to justify vanity, but hip-hop is about swag and style. Hip-hop was built on style and confidence. Kanye said, "It's in a black person's soul to rock that gold." It's true. I love the flashiness. I love the gold chains and nice cars. I'm hip-hop. I'm going to make sure you see me shining.

I remember when Lil Bow Wow dropped "Bounce Wit Me," and I made it my mission to record the song so I could learn every word. This was back in the days when you could put a tape in your radio and hit record. Whatever song was playing on the air would be recorded to my tape, and then I would be able to play it whenever I wanted. I probably spent a whole week listening to the radio in my room for that song to come in. Finally, one day, I caught it and managed to record most of it. As I practiced rapping every word with Bow Wow, I started trying to do that with whatever else came on the radio. I remember memorizing bars from Ludacris and Missy Elliott too. These were some of the foundations of developing my flow.

Growing up, the reasons that I resonated with Bow Wow were obvious. I was a child rapper, and so was he. But since my mom was also a rapper, she was often listening to the artists that inspired her and new artists that were emerging. Of course, Tupac was her favorite rapper, but she also was a fan of MC Lyte, LL Cool J, Salt-N-Pepa, Biggie, Outkast, and many others. These were the sounds I grew up around. And even though I was young, I remember my parents' sadness when Tupac & Biggie died.

One of the blessings about being from the Midwest is diversity. While everyone was choosing whether to support the East or West coast in the hip-hop beef, Chicago rappers like my mom appreciated both coasts. There was no allegiance to either one because the Midwest doesn't fit into either one of those boxes. Being from the Midwest meant that my appreciation for hip-hop was diverse. My parents were free to appreciate music from every region. They could love Tupac and Biggie. They could embrace Outkast and Nas. All these things have contributed to my musical diversity.

My own experience as a child has helped me understand the power of music and its role in the home. As a child artist, I sold many albums due to kids begging their parents for them in my early years. After my concerts, I would stand behind the merch table selling and signing CDs for fans, many of whom won over their parents. It generally didn't take much persuasion on the children's part, as their parents were already looking for clean and positive music for their kids to listen to. Hip-hop is a language that the church should value because of its ability to educate and impact generations of unchurched people. The Christian rapper is more like Jesus than they realize.

CHAPTER 4

In the Temple

Growing up, I always felt like I lived in two different worlds. I considered myself to be a gospel artist, but the industry never considered my music Christian enough. I was a suburban kid but preferred to hang out in the city. I had discovered that I wrote my best music when I was around my friends who were not Christians. Few people know that I recorded my 2010 "Made You Look" mixtape in a trap house on the west side of Atlanta or that many of my early freestyles were recorded on the west and south sides of Chicago. For this reason, I usually go to Chicago to record my albums. There's a natural hunger and inspiration that only comes alive for me there.

Because my dad was a barber, he was constantly meeting new people in the shop. He would often come home having met a new producer, artist, or engineer that day. Sometimes he would slide me their CDs, and other times he would connect by giving me their phone number. These connections led to studio sessions and even collaborations for music that I'm extremely proud of to this day. I may never understand why God allowed me to be in these environments, but He always made sure I was there. I'd announce myself at the front door; then somebody would let me in. I'd walk past three dudes, smoked out sleep on the couch, after playing 2K.

Everybody would show love and respect to me as the gospel rapper. And I'd hit the booth and record. Sometimes I'd rap in a cypher; other times, I'd chill and play 2k. Sometimes we would watch a movie, and sometimes we would hit the corner store and grab food. We'd often talk about God, and it wasn't just because I was there. My homies always spoke about God. They just didn't know it. This is why many of my songs have lines that talk about street dudes knowing more about God than most church people. I learned more about God in these environments than I have in any church.

So, it was in the studio where I learned how to talk about God without using obvious Christian language. I still remember many of those conversations, and many of those conversations live on in every song that I write.

I always used hip-hop to my advantage because I recognized that it was the key to get me into certain spaces and rooms. I've never been the cool guy, and I've never been the dude who can make everyone laugh. I'm often uptight and serious, and I can be extremely corny most of the time. If it weren't for hip-hop and my ability to rap, most people probably wouldn't have hung out with me or tolerated me too long. But my skill intrigued and impressed people. It made them curious about my existence and why I chose to live the way that I did. They were inspired by my boldness and ability to blend in while remaining completely different from everyone else in the room.

My circle of friends has always been small but solid. I've been blessed not to change friends too many times. My crew has pretty much always been the same. I was widely known as the "church boy," and many people figured I'd one day grow out of my "Jesus phase." I wasn't the person everybody wanted to hang out with. If it wasn't Jesus, music, or sports, we probably had nothing to talk about.

In Atlanta, my boy, Mike, was always the dude with the connections and opportunities. He was ambitious and could always make things happen. He was my best friend and was always in the mix. If there was an event or anything major happening around the city, Mike always knew how to make sure I could get in. Naturally, once inside of the party, I was always kind of quiet and reserved. I've always been the type of person that is slow to trust people and their intentions. It usually takes me a few good interactions with someone before I'll even begin smiling or opening up around them. Mike always believed in me and continued to bring me around, even though many of his people didn't rock with me.

Jeff and I became friends because we were the only two black kids in our AP class. We connected on hip-hop and were both generally quiet and untrusting of people who talked too much. My older cousins Chad and AK were who I got most of my style from. I studied the way they dressed and the music they listened to. They were always keeping me up to date with the hottest rappers in Chicago, as well as a lot of underground artists. My cousin AK had me listening to Bump J while I was in school playing Jeezy.

Greg was my best friend turned family. The same artists inspired us, and we brought the best out of each other musically. He's the first person who inspired me to tell stories in my music, and he's still one of my favorite rappers to this day.

Outside of a few others, my small circle meant that my siblings were my closest friends. While everybody else was hanging with their friends, I often traveled to block parties and events around Atlanta with my siblings. I loved being with them and have a deep appreciation for our bond. When I could barely get my friends to show up for support, my siblings were always willing to ride with me.

I've always said that whenever the Lord gave me a platform, I would publicly give honor to the black pastors and theologians that have shaped my faith. While everybody in popular Christian culture was listening to John Piper, I was influenced by the local hood pastors. These are the unsung heroes who often get labeled as having bad theology when honestly, they are discredited because they are black. American Christianity has taken a Middle Eastern and African faith and severed it from its roots. They have sought every opportunity to paint the black church as theologically inept, often mocking our rhythmic preaching and charismatic worship. I have never believed the narrative America has conjured about the black church. It's where I'm from. It's where I first met and fell in love with Jesus.

Choir robes will forever be special to me. I deeply long for my future children to have the opportunity to worship in one. To sing to the tambourine sounds and to jump and shout in a small church with members using printed church fans.

The fact that the black church is still here and strong should be enough to convince anybody to trust in the Savior. We are the most abused, degraded, and unappreciated group in American history. We've been abused by the same faith that we hold so firmly, but we're here because we know Jesus. And we identify with Him more than anyone else in this country. We, too, were lynched publicly for crimes we didn't commit.

While America was intentionally keeping black people poor, they didn't realize they were reminding us that we were the kind of people that Jesus spent time with the most—the marginalized and downcast. We believed and knew that Jesus would set us free from the yokes of slavery and bondage. We were an oppressed group, and according to the Bible, the oppressor often thinks they are on God's side, when in fact, they are fighting against Him.

My very first pastor was Reverend Marcus Green. He was twenty-five at the time he pastored my family. Being a child, I didn't recognize how much humility my parents walked in as they entrusted their souls to a younger preacher. Many people don't believe they can learn from someone younger. That's also how many people feel about me.

Pastor Green was a southern man from Orlando, Florida, and he loved Jesus deeply. He loved hip-hop, and he had extraordinary faith. He often wore bright orange or green suits, which was a country flavor to my Midwest family. He was passionate about the Bible and believed every word that it said. And so did we.

Being that Pastor Green was young, he had a particular affinity for the youth. He believed that the children were the church's future and that our congregation was only as strong as the children's ministry. Under his leadership, I memorized many scriptures, sung in the choir, acted in many church plays, and learned all sixty-six books of the Bible in order. I never forgot any of those things that I learned. My time at Mt. Zion forever proved to me that church was fun. It was my favorite place to be, and Sundays were my favorite day of the week. All my friends were there. My siblings and I even played church at home.

It was in the church where I performed my first rap. I am forever convinced that a healthy church is where children discover their purpose and passion. This happened because I asked Pastor Green to do the "Holy Ghost Rap" five minutes before the service started. He handed me his mic and said, "How about you do it instead."

My second church home was Destiny Metropolitan Worship Church. It was an excellent second step to the spiritual foundation laid for my family at Mt Zion AME. We were under the leadership of Pastor Bryan E. Crute, and this was my first experience in a large church. Up to this point, I had been accustomed to small churches where everyone knew each other. Right away, this church helped me understand something about the church community. They taught me that no matter the size of the church, if the church doesn't feel small, it is because you didn't shrink it. Though this church was large, I quickly realized that my 10:30 am service timeslot housed my new family. The kids that I had in my children's church all became familiar to me. My parents made friends with couples and people they began to see each week. This once large church had become small and family-like, just like Mt. Zion.

The middle school ministry at Destiny took children's church to an entirely different level. We had a teaching staff of volunteers who all taught us about Jesus in their unique way. They were masters at relating the Gospel to our age group and level of understanding. They understood the culture that surrounded us as teenagers in Atlanta, and they connected the Gospel to it. We had the Christian versions of "Lean wit it, rock wit it" and often had sermon series that tackled specific themes we dealt with in our schools. They taught us about abstinence, gangs, and avoiding drugs. This black church was investing in the youth and transforming our city. The proof is my life because it changed me.

In addition to biblical gospel application, this church introduced me to high-level Christian entertainment. Not only was our choir amazing, but we were known for our Christian events throughout the city. Destiny had several artists that attended the church and would frequently host an event called "Destinations." Destinations was a hip-hop and spoken word event reserved for those eighteen and older. The age restriction was due to the honesty of the content and provided a space for adults to enjoy a night of child-free entertainment. I was too young to attend Destinations, but after my parents went one time, they knew that I needed to be there.

The very first time my parents brought me to Destinations, security stopped us at the door. They explained how I was too young, and my parents begged them to allow me inside and even paid for an extra ticket for my admission. I remember seeing an Asian rapper named Kenny, who always wore a Yankee hat. He was incredible. So many other rappers and poets inspired me. I realized quickly why there was an age restriction. These Christians were honest and unfiltered in their expression. They loved Jesus but were not afraid to speak vulnerably about the ills of homosexuality, drugs, and promiscuity. It was here I was first exposed to Christian artists confronting culture. Poems about wrestling with same-sex attraction, smoking weed, and having sex.

All the pieces were rollercoasters. They were dramatic, humorous, and even sad. But they all offered a beautiful picture of Christ. And I knew that this was the kind of artist that I was called to be. My parents snuck me into every Destinations event after that. I didn't miss one. And after every Destinations event, I would go back home and write about my difficult struggles as a teenager. I began to write pieces about sex and drugs. I began allowing myself to be more honest and raw. This was when my content started changing from simple Jesus rap verses to stories about my teenage life. I'm grateful for Destiny and Destinations. I'm a product of the black church.

My third church home was World Changers Church International, led by Dr. Creflo Dollar. He was the first pastor that helped me grasp the fullness of the Gospel, and it has been sad to see how many Christians have dishonored him. I served in the teen ministry and was a direct witness to the work the Lord was doing there. My father was a student in Creflo's leadership class, and my own two eyes saw the families whose lives were being transformed by the Gospel in this church. This was my first experience being part of a megachurch. There were many new challenges being part of a church this big, but my earlier point remains. The church quickly became smaller as long as I remained intentional about building relationships. For those who were not active contributors to the ministry, I cannot say the same.

One of the things that I loved about Creflo was his honesty and demeanor. He was aware of how the public perceived him but never allowed it to throw him off course. There were times when we had news reporters and journalists in the crowd heckling and seeking to disrupt the service. Yet, Creflo would continue to preach the word, teaching us scripture after scripture about Jesus and the finished work of the cross. He was the first pastor and leader that I ever saw admit his theological errors. There were times in service where he acknowledged that the Lord had matured him past a particular perspective and then would proceed by correcting his teaching. He always emphasized the importance of being a student of the Bible and knowing God for ourselves.

Being a member of World Changers Church was the first time I was exposed to how divided the body of Christ can be. I quickly noticed that the majority that criticized my church and pastor were other Christians who had never listened to Creflo for themselves. They were content believing what others, who also had never listened to him, told them.

I've lost many opportunities and listeners due to my history and honor of Creflo Dollar. While I don't stand by everything he says, this is the same approach I have towards any pastor or human for that matter. Let the fruit of my life bear witness to the teaching I have been impacted by. The black church has shaped me into the man that I am today. Life is short, but eternity is forever.

In addition to great churches, the Lord has blessed me with some great experiences. I've been in rooms with some of the most famous artists in the world. I've held conversations and shook hands with many people. But since we live in a time where people only believe what they see on social media, many people doubt my industry experience. I've had the privilege to work in three important industries in music: radio, record label, and recording studio.

My first industry opportunity came in July 2012. I was a student at Howard University, and much of the campus recognized me as "The Gospel Rapper." I was also a member of GrammyU, which was a society of music professionals on campus. When a friend encouraged me to apply for a media relations internship at Atlantic Records, I knew it was a huge opportunity. The publicity manager was a Howard alum and was specifically looking for a black college male to take the position. This is precisely because there is a huge lack of diversity in music's media departments. It is usually white women who make up most of these offices, and there is a shortage of black faces working in the press. The narrative of Black urban music is hardly told by its people. As a person who cares about hip-hop culture and the narrative presented to the world, this position meant a lot to me. The only drawback was that this position was looking for someone who was not a musician. It had been a common strategy for artists to work for the record label while secretly desiring to secure a recording contract for themselves. I knew that taking the position would temporarily put my career on hold, but I was confident that the knowledge I would gain from the experience was worth it.

This internship required moving to New York City for the summer and working in the Atlantic Records office. I arranged a temporary living situation with some friends in Staten Island and set my heart to learning everything I could about record labels.

Every morning I would wake up at 4:45 am for the long trip to Manhattan. I would catch the S46 or S48 bus from West Brighton to St. George and then take the ferry boat to the city. From there, I took the 1 train to my office in Midtown. I wanted to be there early every morning, at my desk, and ready for anything that the day required.

Once at work, I would immerse myself in logging media coverage, writing press releases, and deciding which photos would be best for publications. The other publicists would be listening to music while working, and I enjoyed getting to hear upcoming albums and unreleased singles before the rest of the world. After a long day of work, we would often have a listening party to attend or a private press event happening somewhere around the city. This allowed me to mingle with many of the world's top journalists, celebrities, and media moguls. I met many amazing people at these events, and the amount of experience I gained in this short time was immeasurable. My countless number of awkward encounters with celebrities are more than I can count. I'll never forget the day Wiz Khalifa made four entire floors smell like weed or the day Jeezy became vice-president, and I had an awkward elevator ride with him. From picking up Flo Rida's dry-cleaning to watching Unsung episodes in the main office, I am incredibly grateful for everything I learned at Atlantic records. My bosses Syd & Jason always took care of me, and because I worked so hard, they often gave me special jobs they didn't give to other interns.

I worked hard every day, and my one regret is that I didn't network as much as I should have. It was my first internship, and I was also nervous that they would kick me out if they discovered that I was an artist. This prevented me from building certain relationships at the time. But, more than anything, I learned the basics of PR and media relations and how important it is to an artists' success. I was even able to go on a full press tour with TI and Tiny that concluded with me chilling in the green room at Jimmy Fallon.

My second industry opportunity came exactly a year later, in 2013. I was back home in Atlanta for the summer and unsure of how I would afford my next year of college. I was a frequent visitor at the Atlanta Hot 107.9 music Mondays, and my mom was working down the street with Greg Street on V103. She was always encouraging me to apply for an internship at the radio station, and one day she came home with word that they finally had an opening. I quickly applied and landed an internship as a producer for Big Tigger's radio show. Big Tigger is a hip-hop pioneer, and I was very excited to be part of his team.

Every day I would take the Cobb County bus from Marietta to Art Center station, where I would then transfer and catch the Marta train to Midtown. Upon arrival, I would immediately make my way to the newsroom and begin searching for any breaking or exciting news that would be relevant to our targeted demographic. Over time, I learned Tigger's personality and the kind of stories that meant the most to him. We both loved hip-hop, sneakers and had similar interests, so this wasn't hard for me to do. After compiling about 30 stories each day, I'd lay them on Tigger's desk and await his arrival. I made sure to put the most likely stories that he would present on top. This trained me to keep an ear in the streets and taught me how to stay relevant. After the show was prepped and planned, we'd then head into the studio, where I would work the soundboard with his assistant Patricia. Because Tigger was a celebrity and huge in hip-hop culture, he knew everybody. Every day a new artist or celebrity would come in to be interviewed on the show and hang out with us. So not only did I get to meet a lot of cool people, but I also got to study the Interviews.

I observed how artists promoted their upcoming projects and creative endeavors. I was learning how to professionally answer questions while still being entertaining and engaging. I also was in charge of answering the phones and giving away our promotions and free tickets to the 103rd caller. As this was now my second job in the music industry, I was beginning to realize how much the industry felt like a family. A lot of the same people I had run into in the offices in New York were the same people I was now meeting at the radio station in Atlanta. Everybody knew each other, and the circle was very small. At Atlantic, I had been on the front end of organizing the press tours for artists. At the radio station, I was the outlet of the press tour. I even got to witness some organic collaborations happen. As many artists would be visiting Atlanta at the same time, sometimes the radio station would be the meeting location. After an on-air interview with Big Tigger, they'd often head to the studio to begin working on their next big song. And that's exactly where I wanted to go next.

When you're a young rapper writing songs in your room, you often need to find a way to record them so you don't forget them. So, this meant that I was always experimenting with software that allowed me to record myself. I never had a professional studio set up at home, so I used a cheap plugin mic and recorded all my songs in one take using an audio recorder. Eventually, I upgraded to fruity loops, then audacity, and then finally pro tools. It's amazing how good you get at recording yourself when you have no choice but to be creative. As my recordings began to sound better, I started recording many of my friends who were also into music. But I knew I had a lot more to learn about engineering.

When I returned to Howard University in 2013, I had no money to pay for tuition and was evicted from my dorm. I dreaded the idea of returning home to Atlanta having no plan and no degree. I felt like a failure and refused to go home and return to my old life. I managed to sneak back into my dorm and ended up living in campus housing illegally for a semester. I was the only student living in the dorm who was no longer enrolled in the University.

Because I had no classes, I went back to working my job at The Finish Line and tried to save some money to pay my way back into college. Unfortunately, I had terrible priorities at the time and ended up spending all my money on clothes and sneakers. The chances of re-enrolling at Howard University were growing slim. In a desperate move, I decided to humble myself and move back to Atlanta, pursuing a job at V103. I remember going to V103 every week trying to get a job, and nothing seemed to happen for me. Then suddenly, I heard about a studio internship happening at Tree Sound Studios. I always wanted to record at this famous studio and knew that this was a huge opportunity. I applied, got accepted as an intern, and began working in the recording side of things.

At most studios, you're rarely thrown into an engineering seat. Studios work hard to build up their clientele and to be known for producing high-quality recordings. For this reason, when new interns enter studios, they must be thoroughly trained so that they can continue to offer the same quality services. In my many years in the music world, I've been blessed to have many friends who work at recording studios. No matter what city, the process seems to be the same. Earn your stripes by assisting the lead engineers and stick as close to them as possible. Study their techniques and ask for tips in between sessions. And if that engineer needs someone to step in one day, he'll call on you.

My time interning at Tree Sound Studio was a valuable part of my journey. Many of the mundane and everyday tasks assigned to me were my proving grounds for being a successful artist in the industry. I was privileged to serve some of the biggest artists of my generation. Cleaning up after, serving fresh coffee, and going on food runs for celebrities helped build the character that I have today. The Lord was teaching me how to respect, love, and honor artists who were already in the positions I aspired to be in. I also knew He positioned me there to be a silent prayer warrior—consistently interceding on behalf of the many artists that I was around.

My demeanor was quiet and inquisitive. I understood that being in the studio was never about me and always worked to make sure that the artists felt comfortable and free to be creative. Celebrities have lives where it's hard for them to know who to trust. They also are constantly bombarded with people who want autographs and pictures, and it was my job to make sure they felt like the studio was a place where they could relax. With this posture, I quickly learned that many artists desire friendship and conversation that is not focused on music. They wanted to be seen as real people. They desired to escape the chaos of their celebrity lives.

The industry pressure was immense, and often that pressure is what led them to the studio. The pressure of feeling like you are in a race against the artist working across the hall in the next studio, feeling like you are only as valuable as the next song that you create. Sometimes even wishing that you didn't have to turn in an album. So many artists were here in the studio, carrying immense pressure and fears. My proximity to artists carrying these fears allowed me to see things the world was often shielded from.

The studio has a certain etiquette and way of coping with these fears. It's often the place where drugs, sex, and ego collide. Artists would assemble to the studio with a bunch of their closest friends. This made them feel safe, cool, and valuable. Being in a room with a bunch of people that are dependent on you will make any person feel valuable. However, it is a false value that fades the moment you are back to being alone. The drugs are there for several reasons. They are socially acceptable, but they also make artists feel like they are creative. It makes them feel detached from their problems, and their self-confidence increases. Having groupies around makes the artist feel desired and guarantees a sexual partner. These things have become so common that many artists can't imagine recording without them. When they are left alone with their thoughts and themselves, they are empty and alone—wondering if they would be loved and cared for without the fame.

In the midst of all of this, I was there. Making myself available to artists and praying for them to discover how much Jesus loved them. Many of these artists believed that they didn't have to respect me because I was an intern. Sometimes I was talked down to or commanded to run errands for them. At times, it was so bad that even the groupies were disrespectful to me. It was only by the strength of God that I was able to maintain my cool in those situations. I knew I represented Jesus, and I wanted to make Him proud by serving the artists and their friends well. There were even times when I found myself serving artists that were less skilled than me. Yet, I continued—reminding myself that my time would surely come.

CHAPTER 5

WALKING ON WATER

On Saturday, January 30, 2016, I left Atlanta and moved to New York City. It was a move of faith and made absolutely no sense to anyone at the time – including myself. Just a few days earlier, I had been standing on Forsyth Street during the peach drop on New Years. I would be turning twenty-four the next day and releasing my mixtape "Critical Condition Pt. 3." I remember being with all my friends, comfortable, yet aware that I was destined for more. At this time, I was the store manager of Lids at Sugarloaf Mall in Gwinnett County. I had led my store to be the top sales team in the entire southeast and was earning a decent income. I was well connected in Atlanta, an intern at the top recording studio, and performing at major concerts and events regularly. Most people believed I was living the dream, but I wasn't satisfied.

I always bring in the new year by fasting and praying for direction and guidance. It had been two weeks since the new year started, and I was only eating fruits and vegetables.

I was sitting in my room on January 15 when the Lord told me to move to New York. As I stared at the city map on my phone, I was deeply afraid. I had always felt that Atlanta would be my permanent home. The only other place I had ever considered settling in was Chicago. But it was clear the Lord was leading me to New York. I didn't know anybody there and had no idea how I would survive, but I strongly felt the Lord leading me to purchase the plane ticket. My test of faith would be to purchase the plane ticket and then to figure out everything else afterward.

I bought a one-way Southwest Airlines ticket from Atlanta to New York, and then I called my cousin. He was the only person that I knew in New York, and he wasn't even fully settled there himself. He was living with his girlfriend in the south Bronx, and I called him to tell him that I was moving there. After answering a few questions about why I was deciding so suddenly to make this move, he offered his place and told me that I could stay with him and his girlfriend until I got settled. I accepted his offer and was already beginning to feel better about the radical faith move I was making. I recognized that the Lord was being extremely kind to me by providing a place to stay.

The next call I made was to my parents. I shared with them about how the Lord was leading me to move to New York, that my flight was leaving in fifteen days, and that I would be staying with my cousin. While most parents would've thought their child was crazy, my parents celebrated my move of faith. Part of me was hoping that they would talk me out of it and say something that would make me change my mind. They didn't bring up the management job that I was leaving or the downtown apartment that I was giving up. They encouraged me and shared with me how proud they were that I was moving. They reminded me that I was in the perfect position to take risks since I had no family or children to take care of. I even remember my dad saying, "If you have to go a few nights without eating, the good thing is that you have no wife or kids that you have to worry about feeding." I wonder if he knew that he was prophesying about the days in the future where I would be homeless and without food. But regardless of if he knew or not, the assurance from that phone call gave me the boost that I needed to make the move.

The very next day, I emailed my district manager my two weeks' notice. I explained how hard it was for me to leave but how I had to follow God's lead and move to New York. In exactly fourteen days, I would be moving to New York, and the airline ticket was already purchased. The very next day, after I had sent the letter, my manager paid a visit to my store. He asked me why I was leaving, especially after having just won another sales award for my team. As I shared with him a repeat of everything I said in the letter, he shook his head at the foolishness of my decision. After a few hefty offers to increase my salary, he finally accepted that there would be no convincing me to change my mind. We discussed my two-week plan and how I would turn in my keys. And in fulfilling my commitment to God, I still ended those two weeks with the best sales numbers in the southeast.

My final two weeks in Atlanta were spent celebrating. It was a celebration of everything my city had formed inside of me as well as a time to surround myself with the people I loved most. My best friend Greg came down from Chicago to hang out in Atlanta with me one final time. We recorded thirty-one songs in two days. I also made sure to party, spend time with family, and do a few photoshoots. We shot the music video for "600 Degrees Below" at my apartment two days before I moved away. I left the apartment keys with my roommate Curtis and took an early morning Uber to the airport.

I'm getting sad even as I write this and reflect on how focused I was on being obedient to God. Today, I don't feel as strong as I was that day, but I know that God is with me still.

When I arrived in the South Bronx, it was a powerful feeling. I was in the very place where hip-hop was created. I was in the part of New York that still wasn't gentrified. And the energy of the city inspired me. Walking through the streets of New York gave me a deeper understanding of the music I had always heard from this city. I was noticing the slang and the accents. The lack of space and privacy. The busy streets at three in the morning. I knew New York would add a new layer to my Midwest and southern upbringing. And its different vibe meant that I was starting my career over.

I've always been a responsible man and aware that there was nowhere that I could live for free. I constantly offered my cousin and his girlfriend some money towards rent, but they always firmly refused. Because I was so grateful for them letting me stay with them, I wanted to make sure that I never became a burden. Because their place was small, I was determined to stay out of the house during the day so that they wouldn't feel like I was invading their space. I intentionally tried to come back around bedtime and to wake up early so that they never felt like I was hogging the shower or being lazy. They also had two small kids, and I wanted to give the family their space. I later realized how staying out late and leaving early might have communicated ungratefulness. I never intended to seem like I wasn't appreciative of my cousin and his girlfriend's sacrifice. I never wanted them to feel like I didn't want to be around them. I only desired to not be a burden and am so sorry for the way my actions might have been perceived.

While I was trying to give my cousin and his family plenty of space, I didn't have anywhere to go during the daytime. So, I often passed the time exploring the city or reading in the public library or bookstore. During the day, I would sit and read a book called *Never Eat Alone* by Keith Ferrazzi. It was all about networking and learning how to build meaningful relationships. And it is one of the books that has forever changed my life. One of the things that it taught me about was social capital. Many people assess their worth by material possessions, but the true value is in your network and contacts. Imagine being in a new city, trying to find your footing, and simultaneously learning how to build quality relationships. The Lord was moving powerfully.

One of the tips that the book encouraged me to do was to write down a list of people that I wanted to meet and build relationships with. Being a stranger in New York City meant that I had a bunch of people that I needed to meet. So, I wrote them all down. I had a list of twenty names and a book full of tips on how to build quality relationships with these people. My list happened to be all media and press contacts. These were people that I knew could help tell my story to the world and bring some attention to the music that I was creating. My first step after creating this list of people was to do research on them and go to the places where I would be able to find them. I reached out to my old co-workers at Atlantic Records, letting them know that I was permanently living in New York. My former boss Syd would always add my name to the guest list of all the private industry parties and listening events. Now that I was no longer an intern, I was free to engage with artists, the press, and executives. And this allowed me to move with a lot more confidence in these exclusive spaces. These events were where I would meet everyone on my list. And by the grace of God, I met every single person on my list within my first month living in New York. God was showing off big time and was being exceptionally kind to me.

I started rapping on the train during my fourth month living in New York. It was birthed out of a desperate need for income. In my mind, I had moved to New York specifically for music. I had already spent years working many different jobs and was determined to not waste any more valuable hours working a job that was not moving me closer towards my music goals. I had sold insurance, managed two retail stores, and also finished three internships. The cost of living in New York is insane, and the prices I had been paying in Atlanta were nowhere near what I was facing now. So, when the money I came to New York with was gone, I found myself living off dollar slices and pastelitos from the corner store. As someone who has always been health-conscious, I knew the food I was living on would kill my body before I even got to do music on a high level if I didn't make a change.

On my daily commute through the city, I would see every hustle imaginable. Drugs, candy, T-shirts, and even street dancers. One of the hustles that interested me the most was the train performers. I had sold candy a few times as a kid, but there was something about the way these performers created a stage where there was none. They saw the train as an opportunity to entertain a bunch of people who had no choice but to remain in one place. I realized how genius this was.

Since I've been performing professionally since I was eight years old, I've always been comfortable in crowds. As a Christian, I realized money wasn't my ultimate goal, but I also wasn't stupid. I knew I needed it to survive. So I decided that more than money, I wanted to make sure I provided a way for the audience on the train to connect with my music and social media accounts online. I spent fifteen dollars at Staples and printed five hundred business cards with my picture, website, and all my contact information. I planned to pass these out on every train that I rapped on. This would ensure that the work I was doing would ultimately lead this new audience in the right direction.

I realized that there were anywhere from eight to eleven train cars on one single subway and that meant endless people. Eleven train cars with four to five people boarding at each station meant forty to fifty new people between every station. I figured if I rapped on just four cars for about four stations in a row, I could increase my chances of always having a new group in front of me as well as have time to stop for breaks, stash my money safely, and still be flexible in case I met someone and needed to stay on board to continue a conversation.

I'll never forget the first day when I rapped on a train. I had already been riding the train for two hours, constantly boarding with the intention of rapping but then getting afraid and never doing it. My body was exhausted from the constant moving around and the wear and tear from the mental exhaustion I was feeling. My stomach was growling because I hadn't eaten since the day before, and my desperation finally forced me to muster up my courage. As the train doors closed behind me, I said, "Good afternoon, ladies and gentlemen. My name is Cellus Hamilton from Atlanta. I'm rapping on your train to earn money to support myself, and if you like what I'm doing and want to support my mission and my vision, any donation is appreciated." Instantly, everyone's eyes focused on me, and I began to rap with all of the hunger and desperation that I was feeling at that moment.

About halfway through my verse, I began crying, and my voice started to crack, forcing me to rap even louder to maintain my composure and to make sure everyone could understand me. I still don't know why I was crying. All I know is that I was giving it everything I had. I was sharing with them about how Jesus had taken away my desire for smoking weed and how His love had inspired me to share about Him through music. I was worshipping, and my heart was overflowing right there in the New York City subway. When my verse ended, I awkwardly stood there trying to interpret the faces of all the staring passengers. Ashamed, I muttered, "Thank You," and decided to remain where I was standing. I was too embarrassed to walk up and down the train with an outstretched hat soliciting donations. Tears were flowing uncontrollably, and all I wanted to do was to hurry up and be able to exit the train.

Suddenly, people began reaching into their pockets and purses and handed me whatever bills they could find. Dollars, quarters, fives, and even a twenty! I was so shocked that I almost forgot to hand them my business cards. But I made sure to thank every single person who donated and returned their generosity by handing them a business card with all of my information on it. When the train finally arrived at the next stop, a few people nodded at me and encouraged me to "keep up the good work." I exited the train and stood on the platform for a moment to gather my thoughts. I had discovered my route to earning an income and surviving while living in New York City. I was officially a full-time artist, performing for thousands of people every day, and building a new city full of fans and curious tourists. I knew it would take some time to get comfortable, but this one moment had given me all the confidence that I would need to continue.

Eventually, rapping on the subway became second nature to me. My voice got stronger from the relentless hours of yelling over the noisy sounds of the trains. My stage presence and performance improved as I learned how to make critical eye contact and win over the attention of even the least interested person. It was as if the Lord had enrolled me in school for how to effectively evangelize one of the most heartless cities in the world.

I quickly learned the train schedules, the pulse of the city, and even which demographics of people rode the trains at certain times. I knew which neighborhoods were generous, which days were most profitable, and how to read the people on the train by just looking inside with a glance. I was making a hundred fifty dollars in four hours, meeting the right people, and also growing as an artist. There were even a few times when people stepped up to battle me. But not every day was a good day.

There were days where whole train cars booed me. There were times when the Lord led me to give everything I had just earned to a homeless person. Most importantly, I learned to trust God on the trains. I had gotten in the habit of practicing being completely dependent on the Holy Spirit's guidance, asking Him to show me which specific train He wanted me to rap on. I would ask the Holy Spirit to prepare the hearts of the listeners on the trains and to grant my voice authority over the loud train noise. The faithful Lord always amazed me.

On July 1, I moved out of my cousin's apartment in the South Bronx. He and his girlfriend had permitted me to stay there longer, but I wanted to be a man of my word and only stay with them for six months. By this time, I had been rapping on the subway for four months and had learned how to keep a decent amount of money in my pocket. I was even consistently performing around the city most evenings, and things were finally moving in a positive direction as far as my music career was going. I would often meet people during my time rapping on the trains, and they would refer me to events or even book me themselves.

With the cost of living in New York, I still couldn't afford my own place, so I decided to rent a room from a Dominican lady I had found on Craigslist. She was renting a room out of her apartment on Dyckman in Upper Manhattan. There was no contract or commitment involved and the only requirement was to pay the weekly room rental rate of a hundred seventy-five dollars. At the time, I was in a very transient season of my life and loved the idea that I would have the option to move whenever I wanted to. I was living in New York City for only seven hundred dollars a month, and she was getting help paying her monthly rent. It seemed like a win-win situation to me!

When I moved into my new room, I quickly realized how little space I was getting, yet I was so grateful to have my own space that I didn't mind how small the room was. I had big plans to finally be able to sleep in, since I had made sure to leave my cousin's house early before the family woke up to not disturb anyone. Turns out I was very wrong.

On my first morning, I woke up to the lady I was renting from knocking on my door at 9 a.m. asking me what time I would be leaving the house. In the best Spanish I could speak, I attempted to tell her that I would be leaving the house in a few hours for work. She proceeded to tell me that I needed to leave early at 9 a.m. every day because she did not like tenants in the house with her during the day. I was deeply frustrated and confused but felt like her request wasn't the end of the world. I was already used to being out all day and had practically mastered how to kill time in the city at this point. I agreed and told her that I would leave every morning by 9 a.m.

After a few days of settling into my new room, I decided to buy some groceries to stretch my finances so that I wouldn't have to eat out every day. I planned to cook meals in the kitchen and pack lunches that would last me during the week, but apparently, this was not a good idea. One day, when I was in the kitchen cooking dinner, Aura, the lady I was renting from, burst into the kitchen telling me that the hundred seventy-five dollars weekly rent did not include anything outside of my room and the bathroom. I was forbidden to use anything else in the apartment. I respectfully obliged, considering that Aura was an elderly woman and probably was wary about her safety. To me, it made sense that an elderly woman her age would not want her rental guests getting too comfortable in the apartment that she also slept in. While I tried to understand her logic, I was beginning to feel like maybe this room rental was not going to work out.

Despite these feelings, I continued to focus on building my music career in my new city. It turned out that having a rough living situation forced me to grind harder than ever. The last place that I wanted to be was in my small, hot room. On the other hand, I was beginning to discover how exhausting rapping on the trains had become. When I had first started rapping on the subway, it was to afford food. Now, I was rapping on the subway to afford food and a hundred seventy-five dollars each week to have somewhere to live. It seemed that money was harder to earn when I had a quota to hit. It also seemed like having bills and desperate needs did not produce the best soil for my ministry to grow. I was no longer treating rapping on trains like it was a moment to change people's lives but as if it were a moment that determined my survival.

By week three of my room rental, I was dreading rapping on the trains and my desperation was destroying the quality of my performance. I didn't have the hundred seventy-five dollars to pay rent, and Aura's new rule about having the light off in my room by 10 p.m. was getting on my nerves. The problem was that I couldn't afford to move, and my cheapest option in the entire city was to stay.

One particular Sunday afternoon, I was returning home from visiting a church service when something interesting caught my eye.

As I was walking down my block and nearing Aura's apartment, I noticed a stack of Jordan shoe boxes and a small TV sitting on the sidewalk. As I kept getting closer, I was beginning to recognize that the pile of clothes sitting next to the shoes and the TV looked exactly like my clothes. Then suddenly, I realized that they were mine! As I ran towards my pile of belongings sprawled across the New York City sidewalk, a deep sense of hopelessness welled up inside of me. While I wasn't yet late on paying rent, I knew that Aura must've decided to throw me out on her own reasoning.

At that moment, Aura opened her window from up above and told me that she was coming down to talk with me. When she arrived, she handed me twenty-five dollars, which was the prorated amount of rent per day, and told me that she was uncomfortable with me living there. She explained how she didn't know if I had a job, how difficult it was to communicate with me because of our language barrier, and that she knew that one of my friends had come into the apartment. As I tried to reason with her, Aura wished me luck and explained that she was not willing to change her mind. Then she went back inside and left me on the curb. It was July 31, 2016.

After sitting on the sidewalk sulking, I eventually called my cousin, told him my situation, and asked if he could come and help me store my belongings. He persistently begged for me to return to his apartment and to live with him and his girlfriend again, but I was not willing to accept his accommodations. I had fulfilled my six-month period living with them, and it was now time for me to figure things out on my own.

With a blue laundry bag full of clothes, I began a period of homeless living in New York City. I humbled myself and decided to use my retail experience at Finish Line to secure a part-time position at the mall. Because the subway was twenty-four hours, I spent my nights sleeping on the train or in twenty-four-hour Dunkin Donuts shops around the city. I used my ten-dollar monthly gym membership at Planet Fitness to provide me a place to shower and get clean. As I worked at Finish Line during the week, I never allowed my boss or my co-workers to know that I was homeless. I never told my family because I knew they would force me to come back home. While I always knew that home was an option, I was confident that the Lord was leading me to stay in the city. I struggled to survive, all while being fully confident that the Lord was with me.

Finally, at my breaking point, I humbled myself and reached out to a group of Christian men that were living in Washington Heights. As I was sitting in their living room, telling them about my plans to move back to Atlanta, they invited me to become their roommate. They gave me affordable rent and plenty of time to pay it. God used this group of Christian strangers to help me find a home in New York City. In one act of kindness, I now had a home and a community. Glory to God!

CHAPTER 6

RELIGION VS RELATIONSHIP

A s an artist, my creativity has often landed me in some unique places. I've realized that a lot of the decisions that I've had to make concerning my music career were not easily located within a specific Bible passage or story. I've had to become a student of the Bible and commit myself to learning about the culture and context surrounding its writings. This way, I would be better equipped to apply it to the world and the situations that I encounter every day. Much of our interpretation of the Bible has been incorrectly filtered through a Western-American lens. The writers of the Bible lived in a world that was culturally very different than mine. Yet, the more that I've committed to understanding these cultural differences, the more clearly I've been able to apply the Bible to my daily life.

I've realized that much of the Christian rap world is highly religious. They are artists who believe that the way they live and the things they do make them closer to God. Generally, they have very strict rules about their art – what they won't do and what they will do. They look down on other artists who don't follow their same artistic rules, perceive these artists to be less spiritual, and even question the impact and motives of these artists. The funny thing about this is that most religious artists are actually exactly like the image they project on others. Their lack of freedom and dependency on the voice of God often is reflected through the music they create. They don't challenge culture, grab people's attention, or confront anyone with the truth. Truth is naturally offensive, and the artists who offend no one must be far from the truth.

More people are blessed by your bold freedom than your religious conformity. If Jesus was a rapper, I believe He would've been the most creative and controversial artist we've ever seen. The same way that He was hated by the religious leaders, He would probably be banned from performing in most churches. And I'm also confident that He would prefer it this way. Remember, Jesus came first to the Jews and religious leaders to share who He was. But after they rejected Him, criticized Him, and refused to listen, He then chose to spend most of His time ministering and serving the Gentiles. Unlike the Pharisees and religious people, these crowds listened to His words and believed in Him. Because of their faith, He was able to do many miracles among them. Even many of His twelve disciples were non-religious people.

In my career, I'm currently in a weird place. I profess Jesus as my Lord and Savior everywhere I go, yet many religious people refuse to listen to me. They often say that my music is too worldly. Many times, I've been told that a song isn't Christian unless it speaks explicitly about the Cross. And so many people who believe that metric have shunned or blackmailed my music. But didn't Jesus speak about a wide variety of topics? Weren't the beatitudes or the many parables that He shared also important? Was He straying away from the Gospel whenever He wasn't speaking about His future death and resurrection? Absolutely not! This is because Jesus *is the Gospel* in human form – the Word made flesh. He was living out the Gospel at all times, even when it wasn't explicitly on His lips.

Isaiah 53 is one of the passages that radically changed my life. It describes Jesus in many ways, detailing a person that few of us would recognize as God. It says that He had no majestic form or even an attractive appearance. And verse three says that He was someone people turned away from and whom they didn't value. How does this inform our image of Jesus as we imagine Him being a rapper? Well, for me, it signals that He would absolutely be the artist that the music industry would overlook. He probably wouldn't have the most star quality, fly-est clothes, or even the largest amount of fans. He would suffer rejection as He writes music speaking up for the voiceless and marginalized. He would perform most of His concerts at neighborhood block parties rather than large sold-out auditoriums. He would be slandered on social media and never respond or retaliate. His approval rests in the Father, and His food is to do His will.

I believe that many of us wrestle constantly with an unhealthy desire for glory. Now let me be clear, that I am not saying that it is wrong to desire glory. In fact, I believe that God designed us with the innate dream of being recognized and esteemed. And one of my favorite things about Jesus is that He never shunned anyone who desired to be great. Instead, he showed them a better way to obtain that greatness: explaining that the greatest is the one who serves. The Bible says that we are a royal priesthood, a city on a hill that cannot be hidden, and a holy nation. These are all things that are distinguished, recognized, and impossible to miss. So, it must be true that God does not have a problem with us desiring glory. But I must admit that at times, I have been guilty of having an unhealthy desire.

There are times when I desire to receive glory for being obedient to God and doing the difficult things He asks me to do. I often want people to see the sacrifices that I've made behind closed doors so that they will validate me. But I realize that that subtly wars against maintaining a pure heart before the Lord. I pray that the Lord will help me to desire to be obedient to Him simply because He's God and I love Him not because there is glory or an award attached to it. Lord, let me just want to be obedient.

While the Pharisees and religious leaders wouldn't admit it vocally, they were deeply jealous and intimidated by Jesus and His influence. And it is the same way for the artist who commits to follow Jesus. Instead of religious rules that serve no benefit in making you more Godly, Christian artists are to be led by the Holy Spirit and rooted in Scripture. We serve a living and breathing God who speaks to us daily and tells us which way to turn and where to go. Those who have not heard the voice of the Lord for themselves will often be jealous of those who do. And their desire to live a true life of freedom will often lead them to attempt to limit the freedom of others. Pastor Bill Johnson says this quote that I deeply love: "We do not become culturally relevant when we become like the culture, but rather when we model what the culture hungers to become." It is true! When the world sees more artists that are serving their neighbors, boldly declaring the truth, and living Spirit-led lives, they will always find ways to keep a close eye on them.

Whether it is to criticize them or to mimic them, both responses work to the glory of God. All of Satan's attempts to destroy Christians of integrity will result in more people discovering the love of Jesus. And even those who attempt to mimic the Spirit-led lifestyle without the Spirit will often mimic themselves right into the hands of our loving Savior. For God works all things for the good of those who love the Lord and are called according to His purpose.

I believe that we all live out of our understanding of who we are. Every decision you make can be traced back to a core belief that you have about yourself. As an artist who has long since realized this, much of my creative work has sought to express this principal. That the very struggles and wrestles with our sin and shame all boil down to what we believe about the Gospel and consequently how we do or do not apply that Gospel to our lives. And even as artists, the way that we create music will ultimately reveal what we believe about ourselves. If we conform to the pressures of culture, creating the music that they value instead of the music the Lord has commissioned us to make, it is because we ultimately doubt God's ability to elevate us. We truly do not believe that God can make us successful by doing things His way.

My entire life, I was always told that I could never be successful doing music for God. Many people told me to take a break from doing Gospel music and to create regular music. They told me that I would be able to come back to rapping for God later, once I became successful. I refused. But many of my friends chose this option. And none of the ones who have become successful have ever come back.

Never abandon your first love. Success is not more valuable than God. Success belongs to the Lord, but many people want God's stuff instead of Him. One truth that I can tell you is that success doing things God's way is a lot slower. But you get there without having sold your soul. I have turned down many contracts, opportunities, and paychecks in order to maintain my freedom and to please God. And each time, it never gets any easier. The big lie that says, "This is the only way and your only chance to have these things" is often extremely loud. And I've never felt excited when I turned down money. Sure, I was proud to be following God, but the truth is that following God is always painful and costly. Yet, God is always faithful to add so much more back to you than what you gave up. The only difference is the timing. Worldly people choose to receive their riches now and end up receiving destruction later. Christians trade in worldly riches for an eternal glory that will never fade. Keeping a proper perspective about who owns the riches that I'm working to receive always helps me to make the right decision.

So when Cellus Hamilton stands on stage preaching the same message Jesus preached, the people who love their power and their position realize that Cellus Hamilton and anybody who also shares this message of Jesus is a threat to their pockets, power, and lifestyle. Now I'm the new target. But not because these are my ideas – because I'm standing for His.

There are two narratives that are often held in Christian hip-hop circles. There is either the belief that everyone who is successful is serving Satan or that everyone who is not mainstream has a secret life of sin that keeps God from elevating them. I don't believe or endorse either of these viewpoints. I hate the notion that our Western expression of Christianity seeks to solve everything with a sort of two-party political system. As if the affirmation of one thing is automatically the disapproval of another. As if we serve a God who is not both with us now and simultaneously waiting for us later. God is dynamic. And so are most things about the kingdom.

We all know there are some Christian artists that have made some deals that conflicted with some of their deep beliefs and morals in exchange for money and fame. This happens every day. But it is not our job to judge external factors as we seek to identify who these sellouts are. We have been instructed to "know them by their fruit," "to pray for them," and to "not associate with those who confuse the Gospel with lifestyles of sin." I prefer to not draw conclusions about people's faith that I don't know intimately, to give everyone the grace Jesus gives me. It's better this way.

I'll never forget the day I heard the voice of God while I was on the subway. I had spent my entire morning scrolling through social media and watching movies on the internet, and now here I was, on the crowded train reading my Bible. I remember hearing God say to me, "Now is not the time to read your Bible. Put it away. I gave you time to do that when you were at home in private. People are around you and now is the time to be present and attentive to them." I was shocked at how clear I heard God's voice in that moment and quickly closed my Bible and put it back into my bookbag. I've never heard God's voice as clear as I did that day, but it was a moment I have never forgotten. He taught me a powerful lesson that day. Spend your private time praying and pursuing Jesus. Spend your public time loving and serving people. Too many people do the opposite and ignore the people they are assigned to serve.

I believe it is extremely obvious when an artist makes music for a group of people they have no connection to. I personally can always tell when a person makes music that isn't authentic. The emotion and energy reveal that these were ideas but not real conversations. Nobody really told you that. One of the boundaries that I have in place is to refuse to tell stories that I haven't lived, experienced, or deeply been connected to. It is a disservice to people to misrepresent their experience, and it also is a demonic destruction of their testimony. The listener will be able to immediately recognize if the story that I'm telling is inauthentic or based on my own perceptions instead of reality. This is also why we are not impressed with Christians that tell us about God yet lack the mark of a real personal experience with Him. In my life, I've been most deeply impacted by the Christians who know Jesus personally rather than the deeply theological preachers who only know *about* God. These people make me desire to build my own personal relationship with Jesus so that I can speak with the same confidence that they do.

I am a man who is not afraid to make mistakes, and I believe it is a privilege to grow in front of people. A lot of people fear making mistakes and being vulnerable. I believe one of the beautiful things is that you can always point people back to God when you show people your humanity. Having been an artist for more than twenty years, I have made many mistakes, and many in the public eye. But making mistakes in public is part of being a leader. Unlike other people, I don't have the luxury of making a lot of mistakes that aren't widely known. Yet, I still have the same command from God as everyone else: to confess, repent, and cling to the Lord, depending on Him to lead me and guide me so that I don't repeat the same mistakes.

I have a whiteboard in my room with a list of important reminders, prayers, and warnings for myself. On it, it says, "Lord, if I am wrong, please do not let it hinder your work." This is something that I pray often. It keeps me mindful that whatever I am doing in life at the moment may be wrong and encourages me to seek the Lord deeply about whatever I am currently working on. Even writing this right now is a convicting reminder to submit every page and paragraph to God. If He's not leading me, I don't want to go.

I am determined to be an artist that gives people what they want while never neglecting what they need. I will never be able to make an album that doesn't have the Gospel message in it because that's in my heart. And if I want to continue creating pure music from the heart, it's always going to have what's important to me. But I've learned that as I've grown, there is much power in being able to control the microphone in a culturally relevant way. To speak into the needs of people and be centered in the conversations that people are engaged in.

One of the concepts that I have explored in my music many times is sonship. Sonship is the posture of knowing that you are a child of God. I believe all of our human ills stem from a lack of us understanding sonship. If we think about an orphan who is reconciled with their father. When you find out who your father is, you also find out that you have brothers and sisters you don't know about. Us being reconciled with our father not only allows us to know who He calls us but also allows us to be reconciled with those around us who He loves as well.

I believe the artist provides the lens that the world sees through. This includes filmmakers, visual artists, all the way down to the street drummer. As artists, we take the heavy issues of life, we internalize them, we let them sit here and gel with our own personal life experiences and what we've been through, but we give it back to the world in a way that they haven't been able to see it. This is why you can watch a film that touches you deeply because you've been given a front row seat into someone's story and experiences that you previously had no access to. You've been given a closeness to someone you possibly would have no interaction with otherwise. Or maybe you've encountered a melody that fits with what you've been feeling and seeing. This is the gift of art. For this reason, I believe the more that artists become aware of art's ability to do this for people, the more the world moves forward. Artists help the world by capturing feelings and emotions in the things that are going on in the world around us and faithfully painting them in all dimensions. Not just in one perspective but in a way that touches everybody.

Similarly, I believe that story is the language of the culture. We often try to persuade people through facts, but what people remember most are stories. Among the many things that leave me speechless about Jesus, one in particular is the way He told stories. Jesus was so impactful because He gave people cultural stories and cultural things they understood, but He gave them the gems of the kingdom within that. And I want to be exactly like Him. I want to do the same thing. This is why I don't consider my music as a collection of songs but as a collection of parables. Even for my album *We Are & We Shall*, I went through and found my favorite parables from the Bible and sought to tell them as if they were a modern hood novel. You have to dig for the gems, but the gems are there.

One of the most common discussions that people are eager to hear my opinion on is the "Christian Rapper" argument. This argument is so small and pointless that you may have not even heard about it. But sadly, it exists. They desire to know if I believe Christians should embrace the title of "Christian Rapper" or if I'd rather be known as a "rapper who is a Christian." If you've been reading my story so far, you probably already know which side of the debate I'm on. But first let me take this moment to say that I think this debate is the dumbest debate I've ever witnessed. And it often divides people more than unite them around the common cause of being faithful representatives of Jesus.

I personally believe that being identified as belonging to Christ is the highest honor that exists. Yes, it brings a life of suffering, persecution, and rejection, but I will not trade my badge for human approval or attention. We live in a world that desires to recognize where goodness comes from. Yet sadly, there are some people that further complicate the process of recognizing where goodness comes from. When we seek to represent Jesus in the earth yet don't make it clear for people about why we do the good that we do, we fail to give them the opportunity to experience this goodness for themselves. We have shown them a goodness that is seemingly attached to us, and thus their search for goodness will continue the moment we are no longer part of their lives. I get excited about the opportunity to point people to Christ as the reason that I'm able to do any amount of good in the world. In fact, many people are not Christians today because those who truly know where goodness comes from are not telling the truth.

Many artists would rather be known as a "rapper who is a Christian." They say that being identified as a Christian rapper prevents certain people from giving their music a chance and that it puts them in a box. They believe that it limits them and their reach and impact.

I think if you believe that someone can put you in a box then you are already in one. I don't believe that it's possible for anyone to put me in a box – unless I do it myself. When people say, "I don't want people to say I'm a Christian rapper or a Christian hip-hop artist because it puts me in a box," then I don't believe you are that creative anyway. Whatever a person shall label me, they will acknowledge that the music is great. If a man knows who he is, he will do what he does.

It is because of this that I welcome the label. Moreover, I allow my fans, listeners, and critics to place on me whatever label they feel is appropriate. I don't believe that it is my job to manage how people define me. Some label me as positive. Some label me as conscious. All are fine. My identity will not change because of the label another human places on me. My identity comes from God. And my message will not change because of how another human has labeled me.

Early in my career, I remember performing in clubs and being nervous about how people would respond to my set. I had a fear that people would reject my music and everything I was performing because they had no desire to hear anything about Jesus while they were trying to party and relax in a club. I quickly learned this wasn't the case. Actually, my experiences have shown me that performing in those clubs and sharing the truth about Jesus completely shifts the culture in the room. I've done events where I've performed my set and then of course the person performing after me shares music on a complete opposite wave. Their performance is all about drugs, sex, and money – which would've seemed like truth – but coming after what I've just fed the people, the audience no longer views it as truth. In fact, it's as if the audience no longer respects this performer as an authoritative voice for the evening. These moments are extremely powerful because they are clear reminders that truth, shared in love, will always shine through. The audience just witnessed something that gave them hope and inspiration, and now they've just listened to something that they can clearly see, when laid against the truth...is not good. They recognize that it's not true and it's not honest. This should give the Christian amazing confidence.

I say I'm a Christian rapper, but the Christian rap world doesn't claim me. They've responded by saying, "No, you're not. You're too radical." This leaves me in this place of not knowing where I fit at times. I love Jesus and so my love for Him will naturally be reflected in every song that I create. I firmly believe that God is not afraid of me being honest in my expression. In fact, He welcomes it. It helps others see Him in a more honest way. Sometimes it bothers me that the church can be so close-minded and not see what I am doing.

I'm a huge fan of where hip-hop is right now. Naturally people tend to be nostalgic about the time period where we fell in love with something. Anytime something evolves from where it was when we fell in love with it, we tend to think it has diminished into something less glorious. This is why many older generations believe new hip-hop has lost its zeal. Hip-hop will always be evolving and hip-hop will always be a reflection of the world we live in. And because our world has evolved, how can we expect hip-hop to sound reflective of a world that is very different from the way it was twenty and thirty years ago? What's happening in America, politics and the streets, is very different than the way it looked in the eighties. Many of the general problems are the same at the core, but they ultimately look and are perceived differently throughout the generations.

All of us have tastes that are subject to change. Especially as we grow, change, and matriculate through life. But I believe that we all have an essential core of what we love and what inspired us to even start. So, before I begin a project, I often return to the projects that made me love hip-hop in the first place. I listen to a lot of Lupe Fiasco and Kanye West. Those songs remind me of why I wanted to be a rapper and the idea that I even had something worthy to contribute. Music has changed, but centering myself on the things that inspired me as a child reignite that fire in me.

The best hip-hop is connected to the streets. And as a hip-hop artist, the older I get, the more I have to be intentional to keep myself rooted. In 2010, I was recording my mixtape "Made You Look" in a trap house on the west side of Atlanta. In 2021, I'm recording in a renovated Harlem apartment with my pregnant wife. In 2010, I was sneaking into clubs, getting high, and spending all my money on clothes and shoes. In 2021, I'm running my own business, taking seminary classes, and writing a book. But one of the hard things about hip-hop is being comfortable with your growth.

At the beginning of my career, I went by the artist name of MPH – Man Praisin' Hard. I was arrogant and cocky in those days and wasn't sure of my worth and value being eternally secure in Christ. Nowadays, my goal is to never publicly applaud myself or pat myself on the back. I desire to never applaud myself by saying, "I'm dope." "I'm good." "I'm great." I believe that the moment you compliment yourself, it dilutes the validity of your greatness. Proverbs 27:2 says, "Let another praise you and not your own lips." I believe in knowing that I don't have to convince anyone of my talent or ride on anyone else's human approval. I'm going to allow others to say what they think about my art. I'm going to come on every record but be intentional with not saying or even thinking about myself in a high manner. Cancelling arrogant and haughty thoughts about myself are possibly even more important than making sure I don't speak them aloud. A person who is arrogant on the inside, even though they never speak on it outwardly, is still arrogant. Don't get caught up on being impressed with yourself. The enemy knows that if he can get us impressed with ourselves and focused on our own accomplishments, we will stray away from being impressed with Jesus and what He has done for us.

For years, I was an artist striving to capture the attention of other artists that I admired. I noticed that the more I tried to appeal to them, I lost sight of what I was really doing it for. Ultimately, they never noticed me when I was trying to get their attention and approval. But I learned that when you focus on obeying God and living for Him, everyone will notice you. And they won't be able to deny it.

CHAPTER 7

SIGNS & WONDERS

n this book so far, I have spoken much about my life, my relationship with Jesus, and a bit of my journey through the music industry. My failures and mistakes make it very clear that I am not perfect. I am not Jesus nor am I seeking to present myself as a Jesus figure. I am, however, seeking to draw dynamic parallels between the life of Christ and my own. This is for the purpose of inspiring you, as the reader, to measure your life according to the faith God has given you. Jesus's ministry was marked with signs and wonders, and the Bible shows us that signs and wonders accompanied his disciples and apostles as well. We live in a world that is hungry to see the supernatural in action. They deeply desire to witness and experience the power of God, and we as His witnesses have forced them to seek these signs outside of Jesus.

I decided to write a chapter about the miracles, signs, and wonders that have accompanied my ministry and journey. Some belong to family and friends, and the others are my personal testimonies. This chapter is included to inspire faith in your life. Jesus is still doing the impossible, and hopefully some of these testimonies and stories can help you to both expect and see miracles in your life.

In 1993, my sister Makahla was born eighteen months after me. When my parents brought her home from the hospital, I was extremely jealous as I realized I was no longer the baby or the center of attention. Then my mom sat me on her lap and placed my baby sister in my arms. When I held my little sister for the very first time, she looked at me and smiled, and I've loved her ever since. Since that day, I've been protecting, supporting, and praying for her every day of my life. She was my first friend ever in this world, and I'm so grateful for how the Lord saved her life.

Less than a week after my new sister was home from the hospital, my parents began noticing her lips turning blue and her face looking as if she were struggling to breathe. They knew something was wrong and immediately took her to the doctor to find out why she wasn't receiving oxygen. A few doctors tried to calm my mom down by telling her that she was overreacting and that nothing was wrong, but she knew that something wasn't right. As she continued to urge them to run some tests, they finally discovered that my sister had a hole in her heart and was suffering from a slow leak. If they didn't perform open-heart surgery immediately, there would be no chance that she would live much longer.

As my parents have shared this story with me many times, it has become one of those testimonial pillars for our family. My dad has shared with me how helpless my sister looked laying in the hospital with tubes inside of her on the surgery bed, and my mom has often spoken about how scary the entire process was.

But they never stopped praying.

They were young in their faith at the time, but they were confident that the Lord was real and that He would heal her. They didn't know much about the Bible in those days, but they had simple faith and trusted that Jesus was still our healer. And that was enough. The surgery went perfectly well, and my sister was fully healed of her heart condition. The scar mark that was left on her chest has been our family's permanent reminder of how God saved her life as an infant. Glory to God!

Three years later, in 1996, my mom was pregnant with my little brother Marky. Everything was going well until one day when she had a doctor's appointment to check on the baby. During this appointment, they showed her Marky on the sonogram and did the usual full-body analysis to assess the health of the baby and any potential problems. One of the scans had revealed that my little brother had a large amount of unac-counted fluid in his brain, and the doctor determined that he would be born with intellectual disability. When the doctor told this information to my mom, she said she instantly knew that the doctor was declaring a lie from Satan and that the health of her son depended on whether she would agree with the lie and embrace it or whether she would declare Jesus's healing over the situation. My mom stared boldly at the doctor's face and said, "I rebuke that lie, Satan," and demanded a second medical opinion.

During the weeks while she waited to get a second opinion, she contin-ued to pray for Marky and to speak full healing over his brain and his entire body. She and my dad also spent a lot of time praying for Marky's future and the man of God that he would be. After much of a fuss from stubborn medical teams, my mom received a second opinion and a new diagnosis from another doctor. The baby scans checked out completely, and my little brother was born with no health problems or complications.

A few years later, when he started school, Satan tried to send the same scare back our way a second time. A gang of schoolteachers were trying to convince my parents that Marky had intellectual disabilities, learning problems, and also that he would need to be enrolled in speech classes due to his disability. My parents did the same thing as before, rebuking the lies of Satan and declaring that there was nothing wrong with Marky's brain. Second opinions, once again, determined that those teachers were wrong.

Now, for those of you who are reading this book and who may be offended by my parents' denial of the doctors' reports, let me speak to you for a moment. I am not saying that I believe that doctors should be disregarded or that we shouldn't trust them. I believe that God uses doctors every day to bring healing and to prescribe us the medications that help our bodies recover. But what I am saying is to listen to the voice of the Holy Spirit. In these cases, He revealed clearly to my parents that they were being attacked and baited to believe and partner with a lie. In cases where there is a demonic lie present, the enemy seeks to wreak havoc in your life by tempting you to remove your faith in God and to then put it into the hands of someone or something much less worthy.

Here's a simple testimony. On February 8 of 2011, I was dead broke and had been doing my laundry by hand in the bathroom sink. I prayed that the Lord would provide a way for me to get my clothes washed in a real machine, and then I randomly stumbled upon a laundry card that had enough money on it for me to wash all my dirty clothes!

Then, three days later, I was $2,717.50 away from being purged from all my classes and kicked out of my dorm. I had been praying for God to help me come up with the money and now I had three hours left to pay before the "Student Accounts" closed. My mom's friend sent me seven hundred dollars, my parents scraped up five hundred and seventeen dollars, and my uncle Freddy gave me five hundred dollars. I was now one thousand dollars short from being able to stay enrolled in school. I had no idea where the final thousand dollars was going to come from, yet I kept praying and thanking God in advance.

Then, the Holy Spirit told me to go outside and take a walk around campus while praying. As I was walking, another student named Nena came walking over to me. We had met once but did not yet know each other well. She told me that she was excited about having just received her refund check and told me that the Holy Spirit was leading her to ask me if I needed any money. I told her I did, and she told me that she wanted to bless me with some money. I told her that I'd be grateful for any amount that she could give, but I never gave her the exact amount that I needed. I gave her my number, and she told me that she would send me some money shortly. I continued my prayer walk around campus wondering how I would come up with the remaining one thousand dollars.

Then all of a sudden, my phone received an alert saying that Nena had just sent me one thousand dollars! As I stood there in disbelief, a text from her came through. The text read, "Sorry. I would've sent more, but my bank says the transfer limit is one thousand dollars. Be blessed!"

I thanked her, praised God, and ended up clearing my financial balance two minutes before the "Student Accounts" office closed.

As I'm going through my testimony journal and writing these down for you, I'm skipping a lot of them that I would love to include. Maybe I'll find another way to share more of the ones that I have from my college days because the Lord has done some really amazing things. In the meantime, here's another simple one from college.

One night, the Lord inspired me and three of my friends to go on a Holy Spirit prayer walk around DC. We would stop on different corners and pray for the businesses, companies, and government offices that were located in various places. We had no agenda for the evening. Just to be prayerful and to move slowly, asking the Lord to show us where to walk and what to pray for. At one point, we had been praying so intensely that we felt like God's aura was physically shining all around us. It's hard to describe, but we knew that it was an aura that other people who weren't praying with us could also see. It was me, my friend Omar, Jeremy, and my boy Patrick. Then, later during the walk, a group of men walked past us. As we moved aside and let them pass, we overheard them say, "What were those...some church dudes?" We all laughed when we heard it because we knew it was because of God's aura around us. None of us had on any gear or accessories that indicated we were "church dudes."

January 29, 2011 was the first day that I walked in the gift of prophecy. I was at a prayer meeting with some friends from Howard, and the Holy Spirit's presence was extremely thick in the room. The Lord began using me to prophesy about the work that He would do in our lives, and by His grace, many of those things He allowed me to speak that day have happened.

There are many other college testimonies that I don't have time to mention, but I want you to know how important my college years were to my faith in Jesus. Those were the years where I learned how to be sensitive to the voice of God and to take risks in faith. My friends in college were people with tremendous faith who operated in the super- natural every day. They showed me that God could not be kept in a box and that He loves for His children to seek Him. In college, we cast out demons, healed people, witnessed many people accept Jesus, and learned to flow in the gifts of the Spirit. I often long for that season of the supernatural that I experienced so strongly during my college years.

God hasn't changed and stopped doing the amazing things that I witnessed when I was in college. He's still doing those things, but sadly, I'm not around as many people who have the faith that my friends had back then. I'm convicted to surround myself with those kinds of Christians again. I want to see those miracles happen again.

In 2019, doctors found a dangerous mass in my mom's abdomen. Fitness runs in our family, and my mom has always been in shape and had visi- ble abs. She had noticed that no matter how many core or ab workouts she was doing, her stomach would no longer flatten out. She also was experiencing a bit of discomfort in her abdomen and wanted to get it checked out. She was not expecting for it to be anything serious. Turns out that the mass was large, between the size of a tennis ball and a grapefruit. The doctors were not sure if it was cancerous but were very clear that because of the size of the mass, it would need to be surgically removed as soon as possible. My mom is strong, and I can't remember many times in my life where I've seen her afraid, but that was one of those times. Sometimes in life, when you're always having strong faith and caring for other people, it's hard to believe God for yourself. Me and my family knew how much of our faith had been inspired by the faith of my mom. We did what she had taught us so many times before: we prayed!

The phone calls and FaceTime that I would have with my mom after she was diagnosed were very sad. She would always speak words of faith, yet it was very scary for me to see her this afraid. All of the doctor reports that she was getting were negative, and it had seemed that each visit was revealing news that was worse than before.

One morning, while I was praying at work for my mom, I kept having demonic visions of my mom dying from the mass that was in her body. Every time I tried to refocus my mind on Jesus, it seemed that I kept being distracted and like my faith was being stripped from me. I knew that I was experiencing spiritual warfare, and I recognized the importance of fixing my mind on the truth of Jesus being a healer. I left work and went to an arts and crafts store called Michael's. I decided to buy wooden letters that spelled "HEALER" and that I was going to paint them red, symbolizing the blood of Jesus. I also felt the urge to call my dad and to tell him to do the same thing. We decided we would place the letters above our doors, so that every moment we were home we could look up and be reminded that Jesus is a healer. My dad bought letters as well, and we both placed them above the doorpost in our bedrooms.

My parents would constantly see the letters and be reminded of Jesus, and the same was true for me and Denya all the way in New York. We prayed every day and kept our hearts anchored in the reality of God.

After many invasive and terrible surgical procedures were presented to my mom, she continued to allow the Holy Spirt to lead her. My mom met with many doctors to listen to their surgical procedure, and the Holy Spirit kept telling her, "This isn't your doctor." Each time, she went to a new doctor, waiting for the Lord to show her who the correct surgeon was. Eventually, she found the correct surgeons, and it turns out that the surgery wasn't invasive at all. The mass was removed without making the large incisions that all the other surgeons proposed, and my mom went on to have a full recovery in a very quick amount of time. She had no side effects and takes no medication. Glory to God!

There have been several prophecies over my life. I've also been blessed to be remembered by many people during their prayer times. I'm confident that I'm only here today because of the grace of God and the manifestations of people's prayers. When I was young, my dad would consistently place his hand on my head and pray that the Lord would anoint my vocal cords. He prayed that my voice would command the attention of the nations and that whenever I spoke, people's hearts would be grasped, and they would receive the truth. Every day, I believe that I'm living out those prayers. My music is listened to in ninety different countries, and I've noticed how many people naturally pay attention whenever I use my voice. The Lord is faithful.

I'll never forget the day when a stranger prophesied about my music career in 2015. I was visiting a prophetic church on the south side of Atlanta on this particular day. I was wearing a blue button-up shirt and had my afro fully blown out. As I walked in, confident that the Lord had led me to this assembly, I became nervous and found a nice hidden seat in the back of the church. I knew this church flowed deeply in the

CHAPTER 7 SIGNS & WONDERS

gifts of the Spirit and wanted to be close to the exit in case I had to leave early for work. I remember lifting my hands as high as I could during praise and worship, fully surrendered and pressing into God. I could tell He was present with us and was charged up by the faith of the members around me.

Immediately after praise and worship ended, one of the pastors came on stage and called me out. He grabbed the mic and said, "Young man in the blue shirt with the afro way in the back. God has a Word for you today." My heart immediately leapt and sank at the same time. I was nervous because I knew that that was why the Lord had led me to visit that church that day, but I also didn't think it would happen that suddenly. I had only been there for twenty-five minutes so far.

"The Lord recognizes that you are frustrated because you've been working really hard on your music and haven't seen anything paying off yet. You question whether what you are doing is making an impact for the kingdom, and you often wonder if the direction you are moving in is correct. The Lord wants you to know that there are people in other countries, that you've never met, who listen to your music and have been impacted by what you've written. God is going to elevate you in the music industry in His perfect timing. Don't worry about what people say about you and the criticism that you'll receive from even those close to you. God is going to make your name great, and you are going to point many people to Jesus by your faith and obedience. Don't give up!"

The entire time He was speaking to me, I couldn't breathe. My heart was pounding, and I was processing every word that he said to me. No one in this entire church knew me and certainly not this pastor. I had never been to this church before. And what was so cool about the experience was that once the pastor finished speaking what He had received from the Lord to say to me, he immediately just called out someone else from the crowd. He didn't even try to confirm or check with me to see

105

if what he spoke was correct. He was fully confident in what He had heard from the Lord.

That day served as a real faith booster for me. It was a moment that I'll never forget, and it was also a moment where I realized how deeply the Lord loved me. God was completely aware of my deepest feelings – even ones that I had subconsciously suppressed. On the outside, I was a confident Christian rapper, but on the inside, God knew I was afraid and insecure. I wrote that prophecy down and have reflected on it many times since that day. It has kept me going on many days when the music industry hasn't acknowledged me in the ways that I deserve. It has also challenged my faith, asking me do I believe God's promise or what I currently see with my eyes. I choose to trust God.

Yesterday morning, I was reading chapter two of *It's Happening* by William McDowell. I started this book three days ago and have been blessed tremendously already. The book is full of so many testimonies and reminders of God's love. Every page has made my heart yearn to be more intimate with God. I can hardly read an entire page without having to pause, lift my hands, and worship God. I've even had moments where my body begins to shake uncontrollably as I'm reading it. The stories about what the Lord is doing at a church in Orlando remind me that the Lord can do the same thing right where I live in Harlem.

When I was reading chapter two yesterday, I suddenly began praying in tongues and crying out to the Lord. This went on for about fifteen minutes as I just continued to pray in the Spirit, completely unaware of what I was saying. I haven't been praying in tongues consistently since I was in college, so this moment with the Lord was extra special for me. As I was praying, I saw vivid images in my mind. Sometimes they were people I knew and sometimes they were the faces of strangers. Sometimes they were situations and circumstances I was familiar with. Others were of things I knew nothing about.

One of the images that came to my mind as I was praying in tongues was of my little brother Myles. He's currently a college basketball player for a small junior college in North Carolina. In this vision, I just kept seeing him shoot three pointers nonstop. It was impossible for him to miss, and every shot was all net! Out of the many visions that came to my head while praying in tongues, this one was the clearest.

Later that day, my little brother texted the group chat saying he had an amazing game. He had scored twenty-one points, and six of them were three pointers. Wow! I immediately was in awe of God. The Lord had me praying for my brother's shooting without even knowing that he had a game. Glory to God! And I'm sharing this testimony because it is an invitation for both me and you. Let's press into God and spend time seeking His face. Let's be intentional with wanting to know Him deeper. Let's allow Him to lead and guide our prayers. He is faithful!

For many years of my life, I struggled with pornography. It seemed like I was in a never-ending cycle of being clean for a few weeks or months before eventually falling back into it. I was hearing the stories from people who had gotten free, but my own failures eventually caused me to doubt the testimonies of others. I started believing that there was no such thing as a man who was completely free from pornography or lust. I was convinced it didn't exist. I was believing the doctrine of Satan. I was completely deceived.

I've been free from porn for over three years. I can't even remember the last time that it was a temptation for me. There's no way I can take credit for this. It is a miracle and completely owed to Jesus.

I now realize that I could've been free an entire decade ago, but the truth is that I didn't understand then what I understand today. Growing up in the church, I never realized how callous I had grown towards the Gospel. I knew that Jesus saved me through His death on the cross, but because it had been taught to me as a child, I lacked the knowledge and depth of what His sacrifice actually meant. In a way, I had become like the children of Israel – spoiled by my access and knowledge of God. Because I always had known God, I had no desperation or experience about a life void of Him. I lacked appreciation and zeal, both of which are needed to trust wholeheartedly in Jesus and His work.

I had been conditioned to mix grace with my own personal performance or self-discipline tactics. The last ten years of my life were full of me trying to fight my sin by creating boundaries. Don't get me wrong. Healthy boundaries are absolutely important in our war against sin, but they are not what saves us. Jesus is. The more that I thought I could beat pornography by staying away from the computer, the more that I deceived myself in thinking that I had defeated the temptation by my own strength. I would go weeks without looking at porn and feel very happy with myself because I believed that I owed my success to my discipline of avoiding computers. The sad thing is that for many years, I even preached this false teaching. I would be two months free from porn and excitedly speaking on a panel instructing the men in the audience to stay away from the computer. I apologize for those lies. That is not what saved me. In fact, I usually ended up going back to my porn habit shortly after those speaking engagements. God wanted to strip me away from any deception of self-righteousness.

It took good teaching to free my mind from performance-based righteousness. Dr. Creflo Dollar spent three years teaching "The Grace Message." It was the same exact message every Sunday and Wednesday. He taught that belief in the finished work of the Cross and the resurrection of Jesus makes us righteous by itself. Nothing more, nothing less. I heard this message every week from 2013 to 2016. It had been planted deep in my heart but didn't bear fruit until 2018. In fact, I was part of a completely different community when those seeds of grace were watered in my life.

I was attending Christ Crucified Fellowship in Uptown New York City. I was leading a community group and living with three Christian roommates. We would confess our sins and struggles to each other regularly and at the time, I was still struggling with pornography on and off. One day, I was in my room feeling tempted. This particular day, however, I remembered the words that Creflo had shared over fifty times: "When you realize how much Jesus loves you, the last thing you are going to want to do is abuse His grace by sinning. He died on the Cross, while you were a sinner, because He knew there was nothing you could do to save yourself. Knowing His love and what He has done for you will make you run to Him and run far away from sin."

I decided to speak out loud these words: "Pornography, Jesus has already said no to you and defeated you on the Cross. You are no longer my master. You are defeated." Immediately the desire of pornography left me. I felt like porn was completely powerless and couldn't even imagine myself ever viewing it again. I've been free ever since.

The book of Romans, one of the most theologically dense books in the entire New Testament, provides the ammo and support for my testimony. Romans 6:14 says, "For sin will not have dominion over you, since you are not under law but under grace." Don't let the enemy deceive you any longer. Paul is not speaking in future tense. If you read the book of Romans in context, you will understand that this passage is speaking about our current position as believers in Christ. He also says that sin is no longer our master and that we now have the ability to say no to what it prompts us to do. That because Jesus is our new master, and he has freed us from the law, that we now are slaves to righteousness. Basically, if you choose to continue in sin after Jesus has set you free, you are doing it of your own choosing because Jesus already released you from that bondage. I encourage you to study this for yourself. Be free!

CHAPTER 8

She's Not My Type

Me and my wife met on Instagram. It was a divine connection. Denya was working in social media at the time and had a client who was a hip-hop artist. One of her common practices at the time was to ask her clients to list three people who served as sources of inspiration for them and their brand. When her client mentioned me, she followed my Instagram page to gain a better pulse on the content I released and how it would inspire ideas she could use for her client.

At that time, I had made it a tradition to release new music on my birthday every year. That year was no different. On January 2, 2017, I released a music video for my song called, "Higher." Still to this day, it has been one of my most popular songs. And I never knew that it would be the song that would introduce me to my wife.

Denya, who was a new follower at the time, saw the video snippet of the "Higher" music video that I had posted on my page and liked what she heard. In her words, she says, "I thought the song was great, that you weren't a corny Christian rapper, and that you were cute."

Denya's love for the song resulted in it being added to her music rotation, and one day it prompted her to send me a message. According to her, this was something completely out of the ordinary for her to ever DM a guy, but this particular time was different. She sent me a message saying, "Hey, you're dope! When are you performing in DC?"

One of the amazing things about the way we met is the fact that I was actually in DC on the day she messaged me this. I was there for a concert, and Denya had no idea that I was in town. Her question was completely honest and innocent. In fact, not only did she step out of her comfort zone in sending me a message, but I also was out of my comfort zone by responding to it. We both were out of our normal routines. On a normal day, I would've ignored any message from any woman asking me when I was coming to their city to perform. But this particular occasion was all-around different. I had arrived in DC for a concert that day, but a snowstorm was in full effect and the concert was abruptly cancelled. This meant that I would be using my day to respond to anyone who was reaching out to me about ticket refunds and rescheduled dates. That situation was the reason I responded to Denya's message. I was under the impression that she had purchased a ticket to the concert and was now trying to find out about the alternate date that I'd be performing.

At this particular moment that I was responding to her message, I was hanging out at my friend's house. I told my homie I was responding to this girl about when I would be performing in DC next, and he immediately asked me if she was cute. I told him that she wasn't my type, and then he snatched my phone out of my hand and started scrolling through her pictures. All of a sudden, he noticed that one of her mutual friends was the same girl that he had been trying to date at the time. Before I could realize what was happening, my friend had called his girl on the phone and immediately started telling her about Denya's message to me.

As they spoke, I became so annoyed. I hate when people try to play matchmaker and set me up with women that I haven't decided to pursue on my own. As the call progressed with me consistently yelling, "I don't care what y'all do, I'm not going out tonight," they had managed to set a time and location for the evening's hangout. It would be a double date at Friday's in Waldorf, Maryland.

The memory of how angry I was at my friend for setting me up on a date without my permission is still so vivid in my mind. I was heated. But I had my reasons. At the time, I had another young woman that I was interested in. I also have always been opposed to dating women that discover my music before we build a genuine friendship. I was aware of how much the music appeal could attract women yet how much of a shaky foundation that was. I desired a woman that would love me for who I genuinely was – not because I was an artist.

To further communicate my sentiments, I decided to dress as horribly as I possibly could on this double date. I was determined to show Denya that the artist side of me was only one small piece of the complex man that I was.

When I arrived at the restaurant, my homies made sure that I had a seat right next to Denya. I started off being extremely dry and short with her and not really giving her a lot of enthusiasm in my conversation. But the more we talked, the more her answers intrigued me. We had been talking for an entire hour, and she had not once asked me about my music. She was talking to me like a person who cared about getting to know me, and I appreciated it a lot. The entire evening sped by, and I ended the night by walking her to her car. I ended up even catching her from falling when she slipped on some ice from the snowstorm that was happening outside. She rolled her window down, and I smoothly asked her for her number. Being from Atlanta, I grew up asking women for their phone numbers as sort of a status symbol. Sometimes it wasn't even to give them a call but just to know that you actually could call if you wanted to – that you were able to get the number. But the funny thing about that night was that I never expected to see Denya again. God had other plans.

As a young single man at that time, I had believed many cultural lies that I didn't realize were destroying me. I had fallen into the delusion that real life was the same as Instagram – that the next beautiful woman was always a swipe away. Believing this made it impossible for me to ever deeply consider a serious relationship with any one woman. Even if I liked a woman, I would somehow convince myself that if I entered into a relationship with her, I would miss out on someone more beautiful later. I didn't know that this is a never-ending chase that is even more so fueled by unhealthy social media use. The way we compare women and even our own lives to the edited highlights of strangers has absolutely been corroding us from the inside out. And the effects were clearly seen even in my own engagements with women.

Even though I knew that I wasn't interested in Denya, I craved the attention from her. It felt good knowing that she liked me and getting messages from her. Because of this, I found myself in a really unhealthy pattern. I would text her just enough to string her along and keep her interested in me while never actually setting my heart on pursuing her. I was playing games with her heart, and for this I am so sorry even to this day. No woman deserves to be strung along while a man feeds off of the attention as he continues to explore his options. If you pursue a woman's heart, pursue it with the vision of holding it for eternity. A woman's heart is delicate. Love hard or not at all.

Another big reason I was failing to respond to Denya at the time was because of my "list." At this season in my life, I had written down ten qualities about my dream wife that I was consistently praying over and looking for. All of these qualities were God-centered and served as a powerful guide that helped me in many ways. Having a list of things that I valued in my future wife kept me from entertaining beautiful women who lacked a personal relationship with Jesus. Without this list, I probably would've had my heart broken many times and had to learn a lot of lessons the hard way. For that I'm eternally grateful. However, everything about my attachment to this list wasn't healthy.

There was no way in the world I wasn't going to marry a black woman. Not only was it my destiny, but I felt it was my duty as a black man. As a matter of fact, the first thing I told my homie when he grabbed my phone to show me Denya's pictures was, "She's not black!" And I knew the woman, along with everything else on my list, would be black. I went to Howard University. My mom was black. I grew up in the racist south. This was no question. *Next!*

I would probably still be playing games with Denya today if it wasn't for her intentionally confronting me. I believe the trajectory of many relationships is only seen at the dissipation of it – when you are forced to imagine life without it. One day, Denya and I happened to both be in Chicago at the same time for a Christian conference. We grabbed some food together, and it was here that she called me out for stringing her along. She explained how all of my messages were unclear and wanted to know whether I had any plan on being serious or whether I was going to keep wasting her time.

I wasn't man enough to tell her the truth. In fact, in that moment I realized I wasn't a man at all. I hadn't been honest enough to tell her that I wasn't interested in her, yet wasn't confident that ending our communication was what I wanted either. Here she was giving me an opportunity to be honest and once again, I wasn't able to do it. But I'm forever grateful for that day and that moment when she confronted me. Ending our relationship simply because she didn't look like how I imagined my wife looking now seemed small. I wasn't ready to cut her off. But I knew I needed some time to pray and think about everything.

I ended up telling her that I needed more time with her to determine if we were supposed to be together. But this time, I added some clarity. I shared with her about how we needed to hang out in New York City in a different setting than usual and be intentional to get to know each other. When I finally escaped this tense conversation and got back home, the Lord began to show me my heart.

Those many months of texting Denya on and off had allowed me to be introduced to who she was as a distant friend. She was everything on my list, but she didn't have the curly natural hair that I wanted. She didn't have the chocolate skin that I had imagined in my head. I knew that there were other women out there that matched what I was looking for, but I also realized that there always would be. The Lord began to show me that the strength of commitment isn't seen when there are no options but when there is an abundance of options. That is precisely what makes it commitment – that you are actually saying, "Even though there will always be other and maybe even better options, I still choose you."

Coming off of our last conversation, I knew that the next time me and Denya hung out would be the defining moment. I decided to approach this date going all in. I needed to be fair to her and truly posture myself as a man who was actually considering her as my future wife. And so I did. We went out to a sip and paint in the city and had plenty of time to talk as we sat next to each other painting. We talked about God, purpose, our goals and values. We had an amazing time. A perfect date. Yet I still wasn't convinced.

I returned home knowing that I needed to give her an answer immediately. Time was up for the games, and I had to stick to my word that

I would let her know if I saw a future for us or not. I knew I liked her, yet my mind continued to bring up our differences. I remembered that one of our conversations that night had revealed that we differed on the types of foods we liked. So I decided to use that difference as the deciding factor. Tomorrow, I planned to call and tell her that we had no future. It was finally settled.

When my roommates came home that night, they asked me how the date went, and I told them it was great. I bragged about the evening and how great the conversation had been. Then I told them that I was going to call her tomorrow and tell her that it had been fun but that we had no future together.

Of course, they were extremely confused. Especially when they found out that it was because she liked Asian food! But my mind was made up.

When I went to my room that night and prepared to go to sleep, I felt a strong urge in my spirit to fast. I knew the Lord was telling me to fast and get close to Him and so I did. I was in a desperate place with this tough decision about Denya. I told the Lord that I would not eat anything, not even fruits or vegetables. I promised that I would only drink water and pray. I needed to hear directly from God about whether I was supposed to be with Denya or not. I also prayed that the Lord would remove every woman from my life that was not supposed to be there. This was one of the scariest prayers I have ever said and was honestly the first time that I had given the Lord His rightful position over my relationship pursuit. I was finally saying, "Not my will, but Yours."

I didn't know it at the time, but both me and Denya were doing the same thing. We were both praying for clarity that the Lord would show us what to do. And when two people are obedient to God, strongholds are removed.

At the beginning of the fast, I decided to write down the names of all the women in my life that I was pursuing at the time. I wrote their names on the dry erase board in my room and included Denya's name on the list. I was determined not to eat until the choice was clear. And as I spent every day praying and worshipping, the Lord began removing the women that were not meant for me. It was absolutely no coincidence. They were either messaging me to cut me off completely or firmly establishing our relationship as being non-romantic. After three days – and I'm glad it wasn't longer – the only name left was Denya. I knew the Lord wanted me to pursue her, and it was very clear that God would be with me in the decision.

The very next day, I was supposed to ask Denya to be my girlfriend. But I was disobedient again. It was as if the moment my fast was complete and I had received my answer from God, Satan was going to do everything he could to prevent me from walking in obedience. A simple scroll on Instagram, past a few pretty faces on my timeline, was enough to deceive me that I might be missing out on someone better.

Then two days later, I received a call from Denya.

"Hey, Cellus. So, I know we're not dating...but we have been on a few dates so I figured it would be respectful to tell you that another man wants to take me out on a date tonight. I just wanted to let you know that I'm going so that you won't be surprised."

At that moment, my heart dropped. I knew that I had no grounds to prevent her from going on another date. And as a man, I was well aware of the influence one successful date could have. When men are actively pursuing a woman, they do whatever they can to win her heart, and in this moment, I realized that I hadn't done that yet. All of my moves, up to this point, had communicated double-mindedness and confusion. And I finally decided that in this moment, I would respond in faith. Voice quaking, walking through Queens with my eyes closed, I trusted the Lord and abandoned my own understanding.

"You're not going on that date tonight with him because you're my girlfriend."

Fast forward to today, and me and Denya are now happily married. And I'll explain more about how we arrived here in the next chapter. Yielding to the Holy Spirit is so key! He will lead you, show you your heart, and tell you when to trust His leading. If you are averse to trying new things simply because it's culturally different, then you are rejecting any possible opportunity for the Lord to speak through you in those new experiences. Loving my wife has revealed so much of the subtle racism that lives in my heart. I'm so grateful that Jesus loves me and will not leave any stone unturned.

CHAPTER 9

FOUNDATIONS OF A LIFE TOGETHER

Many people that have been following my music career know that I am very passionate about proclaiming that sex is designed for marriage. I have often communicated this on podcasts, albums, and interviews. It is a subject that I am extremely passionate about because I have seen the way premarital sex derails us from the life God intended for us. Outside of marriage, sex comes with so many pressures and attachments that it was never designed to carry. For example, people who aren't married have the added pressure to perform well during sex because of the fear that the person may not continue being in a relationship with them unless they perform well. For men particularly, the heavy pressure to please your spouse does not aid or help you last longer or actually please them. It usually does the opposite. If you feel pressured to "perform" well, you probably won't. In a marriage that has abstained from sex before marriage, both individuals know that they didn't marry each other for the sex because they've never had sex yet. This means that their willingness to be there for one another isn't dependent on the sex and means there is less fear involved. If you and your spouse have built a love based on who each other is as a person and not on sex, your love will be so deep that the physical part of sex will become natural.

Because I know that my wife is committed to me and I am committed to her, my goal to please her is based on me wanting to and not on the fear of her leaving if I don't. It's easy to perform and make sure that the sex is amazing because we are simply reflecting our deep love for one another. My wife is pleased, and I'm pleased as well!

Both me and Denya were not virgins on our wedding day. We were virgins towards each other, but we were not virgins. And because of that, we both had sexual histories that we needed to intentionally remove from our minds and hearts. In fact, one of the biggest destroyers of sexual intimacy in a marriage is lingering sexual experiences from the past. If we are not careful, we can hold our current spouse hostage to old sexual terms that we created in a previous relationship. We can harbor demonic thoughts that cause us not to value the current person, all because we believe lies created from a worldly and unhealthy sexual past. It is the enemy's plan to stop us from appreciating each other fully. Sex does not equal love, so don't allow your spouse to become a slave to a warped concept of intimacy. After all, Jesus was the most intimate man that ever lived, and He was never married and never had sex.

Going into my marriage with Denya, I knew how unfair it would be to compare her to the last girl I had sex with. I didn't want to dilute our intimacy and special moments by having flashbacks of my ex. I also knew I didn't want her to experience these thoughts either. But the thoughts and fears were real. And I couldn't keep them out of my mind. So as an artist, a rapper, a communicator, an outward processor, I knew we would have to talk about our sexual pasts. After all, no one ever achieves victory without first going through the fire.

Doing the difficult work of removing your previous sexual experiences and washing your mind and heart can only be done with God and His Word. Removing these thoughts would allow our sex life to be as if it were our first time – renewed virgins who knew no one but each other. Creating this safe space of transparency between one another where we tackled the traumas of our sexual pasts was one of the scariest things me and my wife have gone through as a couple. Here we are, not even engaged, yet vocalizing to each other on each date that we believe we have a future together. How could we claim to have a future together, where we would love each other no matter how difficult it gets, if we didn't begin taking baby steps every day?

One of the saddest things dating couples do is fall into the deception that they will begin being honest and safe after they are married. This usually causes major problems in the marriage because it makes the couple feel like they actually married a stranger, as if they wouldn't have married the person if they knew who they really were sooner. It doesn't quite make sense to me. And it never did. So that's why I made it my mission to slowly start creating that safe and honest place in me and Denya's relationship. I knew that keeping secrets about ourselves would ultimately destroy us and everything that we desired to build.

I'll take this moment to pause and allow you to take a deep breath. The phrase "safe space" has been so overused and worn out lately. It's very exhausting. I'm grateful that the church has finally acknowledged therapy and has begun to stop the demonization of it. Many Christians are well aware of the need for a healthy place to confess, vent, and be fully themselves. I've also noticed how along with this notion, true vulnerability has once again managed to elude our grasps. We often move in the guise of calculated vulnerability as an attempt to appear healthy and spiritual when we really have just painted the walls in our hearts with a new hue. We claim to want a safe space, but we are often ignorant to the truth of that space. We will only show others our true selves when we are confident that God fully loves our true self. And if anyone desires a safe space for himself, they must take the first step and become uncomfortable.

Many men are frustrated that the women they are dating don't feel safe with them. They question whether she's being honest and authentic. They stay up late wondering if she is their future wife or if she will be another failed relationship. Most of these men have never taken the first step to create the culture they desire to see. They expect the woman they are dating to open up about her life when they have never risked their own image. How can she trust you to love her when you've never given her that same opportunity?

My dating relationship with Denya began with intentionality from the jump. There was a sermon by Dr. Creflo Dollar that blessed me in a million ways in my teen years. He was speaking about how every date should have a goal and an intention to discover more about the person you are planning to build a future with. Dates should not be limited to passing time and having fun. They should be intentional steps for each person to reveal the deep layers of themselves. As more and more layers come off, the harder it'll be for the person to stay. But it'll be fully worth it. This person you are revealing yourself to cannot hurt you. You are already loved unconditionally by God. A person who is willing to love the ugly parts of you is the only person you should desire to be loved by in the first place.

Me leading Denya didn't begin on our wedding day. It began in the many moments where I peeled off layers of myself. I often came with a list of questions that we'd discuss over dinner. I shared stories about my childhood and my deepest fears. In fact, most of these conversations were initially one-sided. I would share something vulnerable, and Denya would just listen. She was being wise. She didn't know me that well. She wasn't sure if I was trustworthy. She didn't know how safe she truly was. But I never probed. I never begged. I just shared and endured the awkward silence. Usually, if someone has to announce, "This is a safe space," it's actually *not* safe.

Most of us don't enter into relationships intending to withhold information. The trauma of our lives often runs so deep that we often don't even realize we're doing it. We may have felt safe with someone in our past and opened our lives up to share something really sacred, and perhaps that person deeply hurt us. Maybe they shamed us for what we shared with them, exposed it to strangers, or even used it against us at a later point. These deep wounds and experiences, which usually happen in serious relationships, tend to cause us to build walls in our lives. We build these walls to prevent us from being hurt in the future, not knowing that these walls are actually preventing us from truly being loved. When you've been hurt before, you naturally begin to do everything to make sure you are never hurt again. But there's no way to prevent someone from stabbing you in the back. No matter how much you hide the knives. No matter how much you keep your eyes on the person. You can still get stabbed. So, trust in God and not your own defense tactics.

I made our space safe by exposing myself. I didn't protect myself. And as a man, there are certain layers that are harder to peel off than others – like finances. I remember the day the Lord told me to tell her I was broke. Man, if she can love a broke man, we gon' be all right.

While many of the layers weren't extremely difficult to peel, there were some that required patience. I remember the day the Lord told me about the hardest layer. He specifically instructed me to be gentle and patient. We were going to have the conversation about our sexual pasts, and we were not even engaged! How scary and intense this was – the road less traveled.

One night after intense prayer, I told Denya that I would like us to take the next two weeks to reflect on our sexual pasts. I told her that I would lead by sharing about my past dating experiences, anything sexual that happened in my childhood, the first time I was exposed to sex and the way I currently viewed it. I explained that this conversation would be scary and difficult for the both of us but that I was confident the Lord was leading us in this direction. Remember, we were not even engaged at this time, but this would be one of the first moments where she would practice trusting me.

I wish I could say that Denya instantly responded in agreement to have this conversation, but that wasn't the case. The truth is that she was deeply uncomfortable, deeply disturbed, and deeply afraid. She responded by asking me, "Why do we need to go digging up our pasts? Isn't God doing something new? I don't think this is necessary." Instead of trying to convince her to trust me, I focused on the fact that she wasn't alone. I reminded her that I, too, would be digging up my past and that we both might discover something that would scare us away. My vulnerability and honesty paved the way for her to feel safe. She agreed to have the conversation.

Few nights sit in my memory as strong as the night we shared our hearts with one another. As a person who is generally confident in speaking my mind, I fully understand the difficulty of sharing information that wars against the clean-cut image I often present of myself. For this reason, I decided that it would be best for me and Denya to write down our sexual experiences and read them to each other. This would prevent us from sugarcoating our stories and important details in an attempt to preserve a false image of ourselves. I was ready for Denya to see the ugly side of my past and was also ready for the ugly side of hers. I had spent the entire two weeks praying and reading the Bible about God's unconditional love. I was praying that my wife would still love me after the conversation. I was also praying that the Lord would empower me to still love her. I knew how important this moment was. I wanted to love her honestly and fully. I wanted to do what Paul commands in Ephesians – to love like Christ loved the church.

I'll never forget sitting in Brooklyn Bridge Park on that cold November day. It was November 26, 2017 at about 6:30 in the evening. We had set up the evening to be a picnic, where we would eat our snacks and share our journals with each other. It was the scariest moment of both of our lives. We were sitting on a picnic blanket right underneath the Brooklyn Bridge when it happened. As our voices shook reading our journals to each other, this was the first time we saw each other fully. It was the first time I was seeing my wife laid completely bare before me, yet still fully clothed.

As we stared at each other, feeling completely naked and exposed, my wife was crying intensely as the flood of shame filled her heart. She was ashamed by what she had shared with me and felt that she was now unlovable. It was in this moment where I grabbed her hand and told her that I loved her. I had never told her that before. I was waiting until it was the right moment. I needed her to know that it was true.

So many of us rush to declare our love to people without it first being tested. We are quick to say we love them when everything seems perfect, but that is not true love. True love is tested and chooses to remain even when the person is far from lovable. This is the foundation me and my wife's marriage was built on. This was the moment. And our journey has been a deepening commitment to that work ever since.

I feel that it is important for me to share about Jesus in this moment. It is truly incredible that God knows all of my secrets. In fact, with everything He knows, He is the One who has the most reason to abandon me, yet He died on the cross knowing what kind of man I am. A fully naked Jesus hanging on the cross bore all of our shame. Even our deep and complex sexual shame. If you are reading this book, I hope that my life story up to this point has stirred your faith and softened your heart. Stop running from God. He loves you. And you were never designed to carry the burden and stress that is destroying you. You don't have to live a life full of guilt, shame, and feeling hopeless about changing the negative habits that you have. Over two thousand years ago, God entered this world as a man named Jesus. Jesus lived a perfect life and died in your place so that you wouldn't have to be punished for the mistakes you've made in your life. And then, three days later, He rose from the grave. Now, anyone who believes in Jesus and what He has done for them is saved and set free from death, sin, and guilt. I pray that you will choose to believe and trust Him right now.

Let's get back to the story.

So, after Denya and I shared our secrets with each other and I told her that I loved her, it was pretty clear that we were going to get married. We had decided to love each other even though we now had confirmation that neither one of us was actually lovable. From there, we were free to be truly ourselves. We no longer carried the pressure to put on a facade for the other person – something that many couples sadly continue all the way until the wedding. While this sounds like everything would be easy after that, that is very far from the truth. In fact, because we were now being our true selves, we were constantly bombarded with the things that we didn't like about each other. Our annoying habits, rudeness, anger, and selfishness was on full display. It still wasn't as intense as it would become once we were fully married, but it was definitely a struggle.

Eventually, after several months, we came to a crossroads. Up to this point, we had been dating long distance. Denya lived in Maryland, and I lived in New York. We had spent the last several months taking four-hour bus rides back and forth to see each other. On top of that, Denya was also traveling to New York twice a month for individual counseling with a therapist in Midtown. As I was sure that we were building towards having a future together, I recognized that we had gotten to a point where the physical distance between us was hindering our growth and closeness as a couple. Despite our efforts to visit each other, we both still lived separate lives, and much of what I needed to discern during the dating phase was off limits due to the distance between us.

Being in a long-distance relationship had disillusioned us to believe that it was natural to always be excited to see each other. Whenever one of us would visit the other after not seeing each other for two weeks, we dated in bliss, never getting to experience the realness of actually being annoyed or overwhelmed with each other's presence. At this time, I had been consistent in communicating my intentions to Denya. She was fully aware that I wanted us to grow so that I could marry her. So when I asked her to move to New York, I was actually asking her to take a bold step towards our future.

After much hesitation, on June 1, 2018, Denya took the biggest faith move of her life by quitting her job and leaving her family to move to New York City. She didn't know anyone here, so she decided to become roommates with a girl who went to my church. We were now close and in the same city, but she was without a job and friends and desperately needed to establish herself. I was so proud and inspired by her bravery and felt deeply loved knowing that we would be able to grow on a deeper level living in the same city.

Within a few short weeks and many trials, I purchased an engagement ring and decided to propose. I was determined to make the proposal special and wanted to go all out. I contacted all of Denya's closest friends and coordinated for them to surprise her at the proposal. I was going to ask her to marry me on a ferry boat with breathtaking views of the skyline and a romantic violinist who would play her favorite song. When the moment came, my life flashed back to when I was a little five-year-old child at Mt. Zion AME Church. It felt like my feet were glued to the floor, preventing me from taking the necessary steps forward. I stared in her eyes, shuffling my feet beneath me trying to get them to cooperate and allow me to take a knee. The last time this had happened was when I was stepping into a relationship with Jesus. I believe there is no coincidence that both times I found it difficult to move. In both situations, I was surrendering. The date was August 15, 2018.

After we got engaged, it was as if the lust demon decided to wage war on us. Suddenly, sexual temptation was stronger than ever. I would often visit Denya at her apartment and our kisses and touches would escalate dangerously. And the same was true whenever she would visit me at my apartment. In fact, it got so close between us that we ended up having to create a rule that prevented us from hanging out indoors. We would sit outside on park benches or neighborhood stoops getting eaten by mosquitos just to avoid the risk of slipping into sin. As extreme as it was, it definitely helped, and Denya and I never had sex before our wedding day.

Now what I'm about to share with you has been top secret up till this moment. Most people don't even know the truth about this story, but Denya and I had committed ourselves to living lives that pleased the Lord. One day, we were reading a book called *Life Together* by Dietrich Bonhoeffer and paused to have a conversation, as we normally did during our times reading together. I was shaking nervously, and my voice was quaking as I told Denya that I needed to tell her something. When she nodded and let me know that she was listening, I shared with her that I felt that the Lord was telling us to go to the courthouse and get married. As I nervously braced for her response, her eyes grew large as she told me that God was telling her the same thing.

In amazement and disbelief, we sat there silently thinking about what we had just confirmed. We were afraid and knew that the decision was crazy. And we decided to spend the next three days away from each other to pray and seek the Lord for confirmation on the matter. Each day, we separately spent time praying, fasting, and asking God to show us what we should do. On the third day, I called Denya to ask about what the Lord had said to her because I now had a lack of clarity. I wasn't sure if it was fear or if God was saying no. Denya also confessed to me that she no longer was sure. She was also in the same place as I: confused and afraid. So, we hung up the phone, frustrated.

I prayed and at the same time, she was at her apartment praying. And then suddenly she called me back and said, "Let's do it!"

Denya and I went on to have a public wedding ceremony full of friends and family on March 21, 2019, but we were secretly married at the New York City courthouse six months earlier on September 13, 2018. After we eloped, we moved out of the apartments we shared with our roommates and began our life together in a small apartment in Washington Heights.

CHAPTER 10

TO BE REMEMBERED

For all of us who follow Jesus, there will come a day of betrayal. This day will look different for everyone but will have many of the same ingredients. And my prayer is that when yours comes, that you will cling to the acceptance and approval of our Savior. In the wake of the world's rejection, at the hands of family and friends, you are one hundred percent approved by Jesus – whom your faith is in.

In my song "Will You," I pose a question to my wife. I ask her if she will still stand by me when everyone else turns their back on me. And this question is not limited to a song that was created for artistic expression. This is a real question that Jesus is asking all of us and it is the same question that we should wrestle with in our own lives. Jesus was betrayed by those closest to Him, and His followers that stayed loyal to Him ended up being betrayed as well.

I've asked my wife this question, and it is also the same question that I am asking of you as the reader. I'd also encourage you to ask this same question to those who are closest to you. While their declarations of loyalty may bring a small sense of security, we ultimately must learn to rest knowing that God has promised to never leave us or forsake us.

The Bible and church history have shown us that part of being a leader is being opposed and criticized. It comes with the territory. And I would like to encourage you to learn to wear the badge of rejection with honor. As you stand for the truth in a world that has partnered with a liar, you will become unpopular. You will lose the support of compromising churches and organizations, yet you will constantly recognize the Lord's kindness as He sends you partners and donors to help you fulfill His call. Worrying is unnecessary, as the Scripture reminds us in Matthew 6. Don't focus on who is turning against you or how much support it may seem like you are losing. The real reward is God, and the treasures of this world must be sacrificed in order to obtain Him. Our seeming defeat is our victory being actualized.

I wish I had an example of a time in my life where I obeyed God and was also able to keep everything that I held in my hand. Each decision to be obedient resulted in the loss of something. And this is why obedience is so hard. It is costly. When I decided to obey God and not have sex until marriage, it meant that I was rejected by many close friends that felt my lifestyle was stupid. I lived for ten years being ridiculed as I faith-fully followed a command that I often didn't see the benefit of. Or when I was obedient to God when He told me to marry Denya. As a result, I was ridiculed by family and friends for not marrying a black woman. Or when I was obedient to God regarding smoking weed. I lost many friends over this decision, who often assumed that I was too religious and that I believed I was better than them. Even when my parents decided to get serious about following Jesus, they, too, lost friends that they had been close to for decades.

Whatever we value most is often the thing the Lord will require us to give up. Money has never really been important to me, so more than often, my tests of obedience have been tied to my relationships. For my close friends that have a deep value of money and material possessions, they have often shared with me about how God consistently challenges them to dethrone their idols of money. For me, especially growing up in a family as close-knit as mine, my tests have often been attached to the relationships with my family. I take great pride in the love and support that live in my parents and siblings. So the Lord has shown me many times that I must dethrone the idol of my family in order to faithfully love and serve Him.

What makes this even more difficult is that every season is different. And in every season, we have a new challenger to God's throne. At times in my life when I had the least amount of money, those were the seasons where money became an idol for me. Those were also the seasons where my obedience to God were directly attached to my income. We are rarely tempted by something that we are already full of. This is why Jesus was tempted to turn the stones into bread. He was hungry at the time and therefore He was most tempted to sacrifice His obedience to God in exchange for food.

Because I have been a Christian artist my entire life, many people assume that I have become immune to the rejection and disapproval of people. They see me confidently operating in a genre of music that many are embarrassed to associate with. To them, it seems that I am so driven by my allegiance to Christ that I don't even notice my criticizers. And while this is very true, a large part of my confidence is owed to the tremendous support of my family. I also know that growing up in a southern, conservative city with Biblical values trained me to think that everyone had a basic respect for Christian music.

But what about the day when I no longer have my family's support? Have I prepared for the days when it will be more comfortable for people to side against me than to support me? When my message of truth begins to negatively influence the income of one of my brothers? Or when my wife's family is offended by my statements, and she is tempted to appease them? All of these are moments where my worth must be anchored in Jesus. I must be ready to choose obedience, no matter what it may cost me in this life.

If Jesus was a rapper, He'd likely be cancelled on social media. In fact, I believe that even saying you were a fan of Him would be enough to get you fired from your job or a major loss of financial partnerships. He would probably be heavily censored, and they would warn you that His music is poisoning the youth. Because they misunderstand His message, they would automatically twist it and make false accusations about Him. Following His message would be a source of tension in many households and those without faith would never accept His claims. Many artists that are much more popular and powerful would automatically assume that they are better than He is based on worldly metrics, while His fans would be pushing Him to utilize His skills to dominate the industry *now*!

I believe Jesus would not listen to His fans that are encouraging Him to dominate the music industry with His talent, and I also believe that He would not be focused on gaining the material accolades of the artists that are much bigger than Him. His fanbase would be highly polarized, consisting largely of those who believe in His Words. Because His Words would live deeply within the hearts of His hearers, compelling them to action, the government would consider Him a threat to power and the world order. He would be presented as a militarized threat who must be silenced at all costs. Yet the fast spread of His music and message amongst people would elevate the urgency of stopping His career. As He intentionally removes himself from the spotlight whenever His fans try to crown Him, His career only becomes bigger and bigger. Yet it is always understood amongst His followers that His mission is about bringing glory to God. When the church gets so fed up with Him and His ministry, they will conspire to destroy Him, even if it means killing Him. And when they do, His impact for God will be inaugurated and witnessed through all the earth.

One of the things that often accompanies leadership is an attack on mental competency. Because leaders carry the weight of leading people to places they would not journey to on their own, they are often accused of being crazy. This was true for Jesus and has also been true for many of our beloved leaders throughout history. In John 8, Jesus has an exchange with the Jews in which they completely disrespect Him by calling Him a Samaritan devil. When He tells them that He has seen Abraham, even though Abraham lived many years before He was born, the Jews become furious at the seemingly absurd claim that Jesus is making. Yet, despite how ridiculous His words sounded, Jesus was telling the truth. This is often characteristic of the truth. Truth is generally hard to believe and can only be received by faith. And because of this, the leader who is committed to sharing the truth will often be viewed as crazy.

Being labeled crazy is a difficult badge to wear proudly, yet a necessary one to be embraced by any Christian leader. We serve a Master who was labeled a lunatic, so it should be no surprise that as we stand with Him and His kingdom, the label is automatically attributed to us. And I think this goes to show where one of our diagnosing metrics of mental health is severely flawed. I do not believe that we should label people who have differing ideas from our reality as being crazy. I think being crazy would be better defined as living a lifestyle that is incongruent from a person's belief. In other words, to live a life that is inconsistent with your belief system is crazy, not simply having a contrasting viewpoint.

I think this definition is backed up by Scripture's teaching that the Christian life is a result of faith in Jesus. When we believe that Jesus has fully removed our sin and has empowered us to live holy lifestyles, then we will begin to live a life that is God-focused and not work-based. Therefore, the Christian who claims to believe that Jesus has defeated their sin yet continues to try to defeat it in their own strength is the definition of crazy.

I have rarely been called crazy by other people of Christian faith. To them, my ambition and motivation for everything I do is understood as being birthed out of my understanding of how much God has done for me. But for others who don't believe Jesus is Lord, my very reason for existing seems crazy. These people can never understand why I choose to create music that shares the gospel and seeks to help people better understand the Bible. To them, it makes no sense that I would reject money, power, and influence in order to live in the shadows of the music industry. And if I was in their shoes, I would think Cellus Hamilton is crazy too!

I remember when my boss from Lids called me crazy for turning down my pay raise and leaving a secure management position to move to a new city and chase my music dream. I also remember when my peers at Howard University called me crazy for leaving college without grad-uating. And even still, every time I'm working on a new album, people call me crazy. My methods of challenging culture and engaging those who have disregarded Jesus often seem extreme to those who prefer to play it safe. But being called crazy often can make you question the validity of those claims. This is why it is crucial that leaders remain surrounded by people who are going to remind them of their identity in God's eyes. I have seen many identities shift when leaders do not have a safe community that is invested in supporting them and their mission.

I can only imagine the weight Jesus carried. Of course, He was God, but Scripture also tells us that He was fully man too. And as people were calling Him crazy, I'm sure the constant rejection weighed heavily on his human soul. His disciples risked everything by choosing to asso-ciate with Him, yet He foreknew who would deny Him and who would betray Him. It leaves me in awe, understanding that Jesus knew He was in the company of disloyal people and yet still chose to love, to die for them. Wow!

The feeling of betrayal hurts more than anything. I've had to learn this from first-hand experience. There have been certain people in my life that I have loved and shared many secrets with. And I've been blessed to have these same people feel safe enough to share their lives honestly with me. Then I've had an outsider who doesn't know me personally become friends with the person who I've opened my life up to. And this new person, who doesn't know me personally, begins to tell my friend about how they view my music and devotion to God.

"I believe Cellus rapping for God is corny. Nobody honestly believes what he's doing will take off."

And because my friend feared his reputation and how he may look associating with me, he responded in agreement.

"Yeah... I hang with him sometimes but not that much. I think his music is too Christian too!"

At this point, my friend, who had an opportunity to be honest about the kind of person that I am, decided to sacrifice me and protect himself instead. This happens every day and is sadly a natural part of life, but it hurt me deeply when I discovered what my friend had said about me. But ultimately, there is nothing that I can do in those situations.

I've had many friends that used to rap for Jesus alongside me. Many of them claim that they quit because they felt unworthy to be rapping about Jesus. But the reason I don't believe that example is because none of us are worthy to rap about Him, and neither am I. The truth is that they couldn't handle being rejected. When people called "Christian rap" corny, they didn't know how to stand for something they believed in boldly. So many of them decided that they would create the music that most people liked. This would ensure that they were not rejected.

For my friends who chose this path, I'm very sad. Many of these friends have quit making music altogether, and the few that have continued aren't being true to themselves. Nothing has changed in their life. They still have a fear of rejection, and they often will share with me amazing music that is unreleased. When I ask them why they haven't released it, they respond by saying, "Nobody wants to hear this!" And they continue to give people what they want instead of what they need.

Judas betraying Jesus is a warning to all of us about the hurt that comes with close relationships, yet I find hope here as well. Out of twelve disciples, Jesus was betrayed by one, denied by one, and doubted by all. But eleven of them ultimately served Him and loved Him faithfully. And this fact gives me much encouragement in this life. If God Himself was doubted, denied, and betrayed, then I would be foolish to believe that I am immune to having my closest relationships turn their back on me. It also shows me that betrayal is inevitable in a healthy relationship – that as we love others well, there will always be room for us to be hurt in the process. But true love always takes that risk.

I'm not going to live my life anticipating that there is a Judas in every group of twelve people that I am in relationship with. But I am also not going to deceive myself with the lie that betrayal is not a likely and probable result of loving and serving others well. Instead, I will choose to lean on Jesus as I ask Him to give me the strength that allowed Him to love the very people who betrayed and denied Him. With Christ's help, I'm able to forgive those who have spoken ill of me and to bless those who have cursed me.

I want you to commit this moment to no longer being afraid of betrayal. Our fear of rejection and betrayal is often the fear Satan uses to prevent us from loving others. We withhold what is owed to them out of self-preservation. And I use the word "owe" because the Bible teaches that love is our debt. Romans 13:8 instructs us to owe no man anything except love.

Consider betrayal as part of living for Jesus. It is part of representing Him well and is a natural occurrence within the life of anyone who chooses to love others. As a rapper, betrayal is sort of my inauguration. And the weight of it is designed to send me running straight to God. Only He can help me prepare for it, and only He can carry me through it.

I'm always amazed at Jesus's ability to restrain himself when people spoke negatively about Him. Ego is a huge thing in hip-hop and allowing others to disrespect you without consequence is often seen as one of the greatest signs of weakness. But Jesus shows us that it is the exact opposite in the kingdom. I believe that most people defend themselves because they are not confident that the Lord will actually defend them. This is the reason why it seems crazy for us to even imagine allowing someone to disrespect us, especially publicly. But the Bible shows us that when Jesus chose not to respond to His critics, they were amazed. In my opinion, I think it's because they were witnessing the power of God.

In Matthew 27, Jesus was accused by the chief priests and elders, which basically means the religious people. They threw so many charges against Him that Pilate, the governor, was almost positive that Jesus would have a response and a defense. Yet, when Jesus failed to defend himself in front of the man who had the ordained power to liberate Him, it left the governor completely amazed. This is because Jesus was showing that even in the midst of ordained human authority, He still had greater trust in the authority of God. Even Isaiah 53 prophesied that the future Messiah would not defend Himself!

I am desperately seeking to become more like Jesus in this area. My human words and explanations have never liberated me or lifted me out of the trouble that they brought upon me to begin with. I often speak myself into a trap, or in my desperate attempts to represent God well, I deal Him and His name further damage. God needs none of my help defending His great name.

The Bible gives us a few examples of God placing His words into the mouths of men and directing their speech. Not only is this the heart of prophecy, but the Book of Luke details that we should not worry about the words we will speak in our defense. The Holy Spirit will give us the words to say in those difficult situations.

Another example is with Moses. In Exodus 4, Moses tells God that he is not an eloquent speaker and that he is slow of speech and slow of tongue. But God responds to Him by assuring Moses that the same God that will send Him is the same God that will empower him.

Many Christian creatives are failing miserably because they are too busy defending themselves. They feel that they must have an answer and a response for all of the criticism that is thrown their way. They are attempting to vocalize and make intellectual what God has specifically purposed to be misunderstood.

I believe that we should learn from Jesus and stop finding our value in what other people say about us. Just because they say it does not make it true. And just because others may believe it, still does not make it true. God decides what is true or not and He always has the final word. When you defend yourself, you usually get hit. But when you allow the Lord to defend you, He is able to make your name, reputation, and even your physical body as if they were bulletproof. Glory to God!

CHAPTER 11

REAL LIFE >
SOCIAL MEDIA

I performed for a crowd of twenty thousand people in my hometown when I was sixteen years old. I grew up saying, "Let me get two dollars on pump three," as I proceeded to pay for my gas in loose change. I've been handcuffed with famous rappers. I've spent the night in the lobby of twenty-four-hour restaurants. I've had dinner with some of the most famous musicians on the planet. And still, most people in this world have never heard of me.

My experiences have taught me very clearly not to judge someone through social media. Some of the richest and most powerful people in this world do not use social media at all. Most of the industry execs that call the big shots aren't in many photographs. And even in my life, many prized highlights occurred with no photographic proof that they happened.

We live in a time where many people's value system has been warped. A person is deemed important based on their social media following. Consequently, we often devalue others simply because they are not as popular on social media. This metric for valuing people is extremely dangerous for a few reasons. The first reason is that it attaches human value and dignity to something that did not create it. Social media is not God and therefore should never be used to determine a person's value.

The second reason is this: a person's imprint in a virtual world is not tethered to their impact in real life. Essentially, just because someone is a leader on the internet does not mean that they are a leader in real life. It's crazy to me that this statement can be seen as controversial today, but that just further shows how unhealthily we have become attached to our internet personas. On the internet, we can be whoever we want. We can edit our posts, apply filters, and share photos that make us look happy. No one has to know that behind the screen we are deeply lonely. I think this is why it's easier for many of us to emphasize our virtual space.

In real life, who we are is more defined and fluid. In the real world, change is often not as quick as it is on the internet – though it can be. Today, one real-world decision can affect me for the next eighteen years. On the internet, one mistake's consequences can fade quickly as a new mistake steals the spotlight. As a member of this social media generation, I'd be foolish to downplay the influence of a powerful virtual identity. But I've also recognized that a virtual identity pales in comparison to one in the real world.

Every day, we lose someone famous on social media. We've lost several just in the past few minutes of you reading this book. You weren't aware because their death didn't change your life. Many of their social media followers have already unfollowed their page and replaced their space with a new virtual hero. Should we still consider them leaders?

When a leader dies, the impact of their death sends waves of aftershock through entire communities. People are left to grieve not only the person they lost but the work that person was involved in. It doesn't take long for them to land on the question of "Who is going to continue the work?" Often, without being commissioned, the death of a leader inspires people to become the answer to their questions. They begin finding the inner strength and motivation to do the work that the leader modeled in front of them. It is here that they realize the leader's life was preparing them for this moment all along. Every great leader positions their followers to be better without them than when they were here themselves.

Naturally, a lot of what I have spoken about is extremely difficult to accomplish solely in a virtual world. While you can certainly spread a message or an idea, it is hard to model a lifestyle online. It is even hard to model a lifestyle in a book. And this is why the church exists.

When I was in college, I served on the e-board of one of the largest campus ministries at Howard University. Social media was around, and we felt the importance of representing our organization in this virtual space. While our online posts helped drive visitors and guests to our weekly Bible studies, they were never the means that encouraged our guests to stay. Howard University had so many organizations and other spaces that were all viable options. And they all had an attractive social media presence.

So, what made us different? I believe it was our real-world presence. People recognized that we were a community of believers who loved Jesus and reflected that love in how we cared for one another.

We were the Bible study that shared textbooks, meals, and financial assistance with each other. We were the ones who provided space for people who couldn't afford to go home during breaks or holidays. We supported each other by showing up to events and even provided alternative hangout options for people who were struggling to leave the club and party life. All of these were real-world things that could never be duplicated in a virtual space.

Another example I have is my debut album. Many people know that I managed to land on the hip-hop charts without any major internet following. But not many people know how I made it happen.

In 2014, I had an apartment in downtown Atlanta off North Avenue. I was working at Lenox Mall and preparing to release my debut album *The Most Beautiful*. I had recently changed my rap name from MPH (Man Praisin Hard) to Cellus and was very excited for this new emergence. As I was experimenting heavily with R&B sounds and was working closely with my producer Neal Howard, I decided that my primary means of promotion would be person-to-person. I recognized that the tool to being effective on social media was going viral. I knew that giving other people an incentive to share my album would go much further than me working to share it by myself. I had come up with a plan.

Initially, since the album was called *The Most Beautiful*, I decided to reach out to all the women I could think of. I printed my album cover on a twelve-by-twelve vinyl sleeve and carried it with me everywhere that I went. I spent my days scheduling meetup times so that my female friends could take pictures holding my album cover in many different parts of the city. I never felt the need to ask my friends to post the photos. I would just schedule the time and place for me to meet with them, come take the photo, and then post it myself. I knew that there was a chance they might post it, but I never wanted them to feel obligated to do so. I just wanted them to know that I was grateful for them allowing me to use their faces.

My logic behind this was simple. And I knew that most of my followers would not know the women holding my album cover. I knew that social media was a curious place and that people rarely pay attention to something until they see a bunch of people doing it. For me, I was tricking the system. I was providing the illusion that I had an entire army of people supporting my album. I was telling the story that this album was something worth being excited about and that if you ever had your chance to take a picture with the cover, you'd then be cool.

As I continued posting pictures of my female friends holding my album cover, eventually, people began stopping me to ask about the cover. They would tell me that they saw it on social media and wanted to take a picture with it. Oftentimes, they would post it and include the hashtag *#themostbeautiful.*

Looking back, I wish I would've known what I understand now. I would've focused on making more of a real-world connection with these people who were posting my cover than just feeding into the facade of being popular on a virtual stage. I ended up opening the modeling pool and allowing anyone willing to take pictures with my cover. Photos included men, babies, and animals. The hashtag *#themostbeautiful* was floating all around Atlanta and eventually the cyber world. My album went on to peak number thirty-seven on the iTunes hip-hop charts as I had racked up a large number of preorders.

I'm using this example to illustrate the most powerful point: nobody remembers that album. But many people remember taking the photo. They remember the in-person interaction. And if I could go back, I would've sought to make more of an investment into those people's lives. For one day, I was famous on the internet. But none of those people would be impacted if I were to die.

One of the things that I've been doing since the start of my career is street ministry and prison ministry. Hip-hop is the language of the streets, and many people won't listen to what someone has to say unless they can communicate in the same language. It's been a consistent theme in my life and something I've always recognized. I often was given access to certain spaces or people simply because they respected my gift. They listened to me simply because I could rap.

Before the coronavirus pandemic, I was a mentor in my neighborhood's local middle school. I also was at Riker's Island every Monday building relationships with inmates and playing basketball. We usually had a steady crew of about five guys that went with us on Mondays. On days when we were low on mentors, I'd share a short sermon or rap a few verses for the young men in the jail. We'd play basketball and pray together. These have been some of the most powerful moments in my life. And none of them are recorded on social media.

I remember sitting at a table with a young man who was eighteen. We immediately had a special bond since he was from Chicago, and we talked about the differences between Englewood and Park Hill, Staten Island. He was eighteen years old and already had four kids – having had his first one at the age of fifteen. He was the baby of his family and had learned how to sell drugs from his older brothers who were just trying to take care of their mom, who had no money. He didn't trust me, and I wasn't offended. I completely understood. I don't trust strangers either. We traded stories.

By this point, I had learned that the young men I meet in these jails live a very transient life. It's always a blessing to return the following week to see familiar faces, but sadly the jails move just like the streets. One minute you're there and the next you're gone. Many of these young men get transferred to other jails or moved to different units. I didn't know if I would ever see him again after this day, so I intended to tell him about Jesus. That's always my goal.

Who you know has always been an important code in the streets, and it was very important to Jesus too. Saying the right name can literally save your life. And being affiliated with the wrong people makes you a marked man. Turns out I and this young man knew some of the same people and that immediately allowed him to open up to me. He shared with me about how he ended up in jail and his current struggles. The entire time we were talking, the Holy Spirit was speaking to me very clearly. I knew exactly the lies that needed to be removed and replaced with God's truth. I asked him if we could read the Bible together, and we did. I told him about Jesus and prayed with him. Our time didn't result in him accepting Jesus, but a seed was planted, and that is a young man I'll never forget.

The small influence that my life had on that young man is still a thousand times greater than if he were to scroll past one of my posts on social media without ever interacting with me. Real-life interaction leaves room for dialogue and even wrestles through disagreements. It also allows the person to experience your love, sacrifice, and time commitment to them. Anybody can walk into jail and take a picture of themselves shaking hands with inmates. That picture will probably secure many likes because most people acknowledge positivity. But I've learned that the real work of relationships is often not picture-perfect. When love is being experienced, the person in need of love usually is vulnerable and would prefer not to be photographed or exploited. Thus, our moments of greatest impact will rarely be captured on film.

I remember having a discussion with my pastor about my beef with "good deeds being filmed." While he agreed with my statement about how filming good deeds can come from an insincere place, he challenged me with his insight. He spoke about how the public display of our good deeds allows people to recognize God's kindness and how it also can motivate others to do good works as well. I immediately agreed and was very grateful for him challenging me with this viewpoint. I, too, am a witness to this fact. Many of the things that I do now are because I was motivated and inspired by the recorded good works of someone else. But even stronger than that, I'm extremely grateful that Jesus's good works were recorded. And in this lies the greatest lesson.

When Jesus served others, He did not do it to be seen or to receive glory. In John 8:50, Jesus says, "I do not seek my own glory." His goal was to always bring glory to His father—who in exchange, brought glory to Jesus. We see this in John 8:54. What this teaches us is something extremely powerful about the way we serve others. I am convinced that when we do good deeds for God (and not to be seen), that He then brings glory to us. Remember, everything Jesus did was for the Father, yet the works that He did were talked about and shared even when He tried to keep them a secret. And I think this is how we should be also.

There are many things that I and my wife do in our community that we've never photographed or shared publicly, yet the impact of those things has been widely felt. This is how the kingdom works! The same way that the evil deeds of men are exposed, God exposes the good deeds of men that are done in secret. Knowing that God is a rewarder of those who seek Him is a promise that we must receive in faith.

There have been many cases of Christian leaders falling into disgrace because of their misdeeds being exposed. Sinful choices and lifestyles have tarnished their witness for Christ. And I've noticed that, usually, people who are more focused on internet ministry instead of personal ministry fall the hardest. I think this shows something important about the way a lack of personal relationships wires us to think. Could it be that having a primarily internet-based approach to connecting with people leads us to think that our real-life integrity isn't as important? That since people aren't engaging with the private aspects of our lives, we don't need to be vigilant to make sure that we are careful and faithful? Well, I believe there is a correlation.

One of the sad things that I've noticed is that Christian creatives and leaders who have a lack of personal relationships lose sight that they have no human witnesses to defend their honorable name. The sad truth is that your internet fans, who have no real-world connection to

CHAPTER 11 REAL LIFE > SOCIAL MEDIA

you, will not defend you when you are accused. Because they do not know you in real life, they have no basis on whether the claims against you are true or false. And by default, they will believe whatever they hear that is negative about you.

On the other hand, those who are focused on real-world impact and prioritizing personal relationships will have people that know them deeply and who will attest to the character and integrity that the detached internet may try to run with. As a follower of Christ and a leader with integrity, you must be aware that you will be attacked and falsely accused. But if you have forced people to only know and receive from you based on the life you have built virtually, you are in a danger-ous position. I have seen this many times and will give you examples.

I have seen many Christian leaders fall under the fire of public accu-sation. Some have been true, and some have been false. For the true ones, there was often a lack of accountability. Many times, these leaders have become so inflated by their influence that they stop listening to the people the Lord has placed in their lives to keep them accountable. They stop seeking counsel and begin to only surround themselves with yes-men. They want nothing to do with anyone who will oppose them or tell them that they are wrong. These Christian leaders fall into all kinds of sin and deception, and instead of working to defend them, their close relationships usually work to confirm the accusations. Usually, these people who are closest to the leaders are often the ones testifying that the leader stopped listening to them and began removing healthy relationships. The leader's reputation in real life and on the internet are both damaged, and they have nowhere in the world that isn't aware of their shortcomings. This is something that is so sad to see and has done a lot of damage to the witness of the church.

In the cases where I have seen faithful Christian leaders get falsely accused, the situation is almost always the opposite. In these cases, their

151

close relationships see it as their duty to defend the reputation of the Christian leader. And because these people know the leader personally and up-close, their testimonies hold tremendous weight in dismantling the false lies. While the internet and the virtual world full of strangers are rapidly spreading and feeding the lies, the leader still has dignity and respect in his community and amongst his closest relationships. In these cases, those close relationships also have tremendous power in expressing their truth and witness of the leader on the internet. Internet lies can be substantially destroyed due to the personal witnesses of many people. And sadly, even in the cases where the internet image may be permanently tarnished, the leader is still able to have a life-changing impact in real-world spaces. It is better to have a good name in real life and a bad name on the internet than a bad name in real life and a good name on the internet.

Let's pause and take a moment to reflect. As a Christian creative, are you having a real-world impact with people who deeply know you? Are you loving and serving people in real life substantially greater than what you are sharing virtually? Are you confident that your faithful witness for Christ in the community would encourage the people closest to you to defend your name and reputation? Or are you living on an island and expecting internet strangers to support you when storms come? If the answers to any of these questions raise a concern or expose that you have built a virtual identity while neglecting your reality, then I pray that you will make the necessary changes quickly.

One thing that I've been guilty of is being an "internet Christian." I've realized that it is so much easier for me to be a confident Christian online and through social media than it is for me to be a confident Christian in real life. My biography on social media says, "Jesus Follower" at the very top! Yet how often do I start my human introductions with this level of boldness? Hardly ever. And this is something that I've noticed generally amongst many people. There is a comfortability that exists within the virtual space that is fake. People will comment or message things that they would never dare to say in person or public. And this has become extremely problematic for Christians.

I had a difficult wake-up call one day as I was talking to a man. During our conversation, I knew that this man was not a fan of Jesus, and because of what I knew about him, I wasn't confident to speak boldly about Jesus in his presence. Yet I knew that if this were a stranger on the internet, I would probably hide behind my identity as a Christian and deceive myself into believing that I did not struggle with boldness or being ashamed of the gospel. The internet has us fooled. We think that we're bold because we post our "Christian" lives and are safe behind a screen. But it's a very different beast to stand for Christ when you're staring into the eyes of someone who doesn't care.

And this is the task we are called to. I believe that Jesus is not impressed with our bold social media profiles that declare we are His followers. He knows that most of us are like me – guilty of proclaiming an image on the internet that we would never profess in real life. Jesus is calling us to be bold representatives of Him in all spaces. One of my constant prayers is, "Lord, give me the courage to stand up for you no matter what. Help me to not be ashamed to be a Christian."

And the measurement of our boldness begins in real life. It is not measured according to the boldness of your neighbor but according to the faith the Lord has given to you. Just because I'm braver than most men doesn't mean I'm brave enough. Lord, remove my fear.

When I think about the eras in history, it is pretty easy to recognize the leaders of specific movements. When I think about black leaders in history, I think about Martin Luther King, John Lewis, Fred Hampton, and several others. None of these leaders had social media, yet their follower counts were huge. And the commonality between all of them is that their platforms were built on the work they all began in their communities.

Their names first rang locally, before they began to ring nationally. And this path towards leadership and influence has not changed.

Jesus was from Nazareth, yet due to His hometown's rejection of Him, He ended up hanging out in the Galilee region. There, He built roots and served and loved people so profoundly that His name began to ring bells in neighboring towns. As He became famous throughout Galilee, He traveled to other regions, fulfilling His mission by teaching and performing miracles. The people that met Jesus shared about Him everywhere to the point where other towns were hearing about Him even far away. Jesus confirmed the order of influence and impact with His very life. He changed the world by loving and serving people in real life, not through the internet.

I've often heard people ask, "Who is our modern-day leader?" And usually, people will throw out the name of entertainers or politicians as their answer. The problem then becomes evident when someone in the room disagrees on whether that person is a leader or not. It's as if we have role models yet can't find a single person that we all agree on to be our leader. Herein lies the problem posed by "virtual leadership." Virtual leadership is highly subjective based on the content you subscribe to and who you choose to follow online. And because these people may or may not have a life that impacts or influences yours, they may not be viewed as a leader depending on your proximity to them.

I believe that in the cases of Jesus and the other leaders I've listed above, there was not as much a dispute over leadership as much as we have with our "virtual leaders" today. While we, of course, know that all of these leaders had great opposition, the recognition of them as leaders of a movement was very clear. For example, today, if you ask who the leader of hip-hop is, you will hear many different answers. People may agree that the person is qualified to be considered a leader, but they will hardly agree that the person is actually *the* leader.

When Fred Hampton was feeding families and children and uniting gangs with the Black Panther Party, all of those people he had built relationships with recognized him as a leader. It's as if the person who physically touches the most lives automatically becomes the leader. Whoever feeds the most people becomes the leader. And if a person who hasn't fed anyone dares to call themself a leader in the presence of those who have been fed by someone else, those people are likely to question the claim. Fred Hampton fed and supported more people than any other black person in Chicago at the time; therefore, he became the leader. Martin Luther King Jr. served the city of Atlanta by lobbying for people's rights as he chaired the NAACP. For this reason, he became the leader. He who serves the most has the greatest influence. And Jesus confirmed this when He said, "The leader should be like a servant" (Luke 22:26).

Ultimately, the reason we are not seeing distinct leaders in our world today is because no one is trying to serve. There is no longer a race to see who can serve the most people. Whoever serves the most will be the undisputed leader of a generation. And whoever serves the most will have the most impact in real life and online. The two spaces are deeply connected, yet the correlation only happens one way. Just because you have a lot of followers online does not mean that you are a leader. Your online presence has not served anyone until you are living out your virtual message in the real world. Because we are in a digital age, the person who has the most influence in the real world will have no problem gaining influence virtually. At that point, it will just be a matter of marketing and digital strategy. But if the people who are impacted by you in real life have virtual profiles, then they will have no problem following you online. They have been following you in real life and will easily be interested in anything that you have to offer in a virtual space.

Remaining faithful to my book's title and proper application, allow me to connect this back to Jesus as a rapper. If Jesus was a rapper, I believe

He would utilize social media and that He would have a large number of followers. While some of these followers would be people that have probably only heard about Him, I believe many of His followers would be people that He has personally impacted. In His short three-year rap career, He would be recognized as an undisputed leader. Jesus would be ordained by God yet supported by the many people He has served. His name and reputation would be frequently slandered online, yet his real-life impact would be so great that many people rise to His defense both in communities and virtually. He would have many online stalkers and many fake accounts pretending to be Him. He would not post anything that He isn't living every day.

CHAPTER 12

SOW AND TELL

As an artist who has been professionally navigating the music industry for twenty years, I often think about my legacy. Many generations of talented artists have come before me. Few are considered legends, and even fewer have had a significant and long-lasting impact. How will I distinguish myself? How will I leave a mark on the course of history? Well, I guess I'll begin studying and learning from the greats.

One of the things that I love about Jesus is how he never shuns us for desiring to be great. In fact, when the disciples were concerned about greatness, Jesus explained how it was to be obtained. He taught that the greatest is actually the person who becomes the least. Who, like Himself, takes on the posture of being a servant. Someone who lives their life for the benefit of others, trading immediate glory for the crown that is promised at a later time. This is how I will live, and this is how I will be remembered.

As a hip-hop head, it kind of goes unspoken that I desire to be remembered as one of the greatest rappers in history. I often tell people that external affirmation is kind of interwoven within the culture of hip-hop. This ultimately means that I must be all the more careful to not prioritize a hip-hop value system over the value system that Jesus has clearly set. But now that I've made it clear where I stand on the "greatest rapper in history" topic, let's proceed.

In September of 2019, me and my wife launched our company Sow and Tell. The Lord has often spoken to me through dreams, and the company launch was dropped into my spirit late in the midnight hour. I woke up knowing clearly that the Lord was telling me to launch my LLC that very day. Unfortunately, fear and lack of clarity had given me cold feet. As I was going through my day and getting some work done, I received a call from my friend Marco. He's one of my most creative friends in New York and often speaks prophetically, even though he doesn't easily acknowledge that he hears the voice of God. When I answered the phone, he immediately began confirming my dream from the night before: "Yo! I don't know why it was on my heart to tell you to launch an LLC ASAP. I really do feel like you're an owner and not just an artist. I think you having some ownership and the position will help people pay more attention to what you're doing. Just my thoughts."

I couldn't believe it. Well, actually I could. Marco had often confirmed things the Lord was speaking to me. As soon as I hung up the phone, I registered my LLC, and Sow and Tell was born. Immediately, my wife began servicing her clients through our company. She was already working as an independent contractor and so she was immediately ready to go. I was still unclear about how God wanted me to utilize the new company. As I sought the Lord in prayer, he began showing me a discipleship model. It was the same way that Jesus and His message was passed down – through people.

I realized that for two entire decades, I had built a music model that was eternally unsustainable. I had been in the practice of releasing great music and working extremely hard to funnel fans towards my content. The only problem was that I had no back-up plan for the generations after me. I'm a human and not infinite. What good does it accomplish for me to build an entire empire based on my artistry if there is not a discipling of artists who will continue the work?

As I've shared in my story, the Lord has allowed me to stand the test of time and to endure many changing seasons in the music industry. My faith and hope in Christ and His resurrection have been the consistent glue that has held me in place when so many of my artist friends have fallen away. I've recognized that many Christian artists seem to only have half of what is necessary. Either they are extremely talented yet lack an intimate and personal relationship with Jesus, or they are intimate and personal with Jesus and lack creative talent. I decided to be the bridge that connected these two aspects of artists. The plan that I would establish to streamline this process and accomplish this would come months later after much trial and error. I'll explain my three plans below, and afterward, I'll explain to you how they were birthed.

My first plan was to develop a comprehensive writing class. This class would focus on helping artists learn how to communicate effectively through storytelling. It would also teach my personal philosophy – that the Christian artist can't help but be inspired whenever they look intently at the Cross. I knew that if I could show people that Jesus teaching through parables was exactly what Christian artists should do, their writing would automatically improve. I developed my curriculum and intently attacked the flaws and common failures I observed in Christian writing. I placed the focus back on knowing God intimately and only speaking His Word. There are no borders around our creativity by limiting ourselves to the Bible. The Bible is alive and is inexhaustible. We will never run out of content.

An important thing that I focus on in all my writing classes is a comprehensive understanding of the Bible. One of the great problems of Christian artistry nowadays is that many Christians do not know or understand the Bible. The result of this has been art that lacks depth and substance. We can't share what we don't know. So, I've made it my mission to make sure that the artists I work with have a deep understanding of the Bible and of the gospel. In fact, my main focus is discipleship. In my writing classes, my desire is that my students will see Jesus as the greatest reward in life. I am focused on showing them that the Bible is not a life manual as many Westerners think. It is instead a detailed book all about one person: Jesus!

One of the natural things that happens in my writing classes is personal healing. Our time spent during devotionals teaches us to engage with the Bible in a dialogical way. Too many times we have approached the text only thinking that it gives something to us. The Bible must become a table where conversation with the Lord is encouraged and facilitated. When we read the Bible and posture ourselves to speak to God our hearts and our deepest questions, we allow the Holy Spirit to breathe on the pages and show us what isn't so clearly written. These powerful moments become pillars in our faith journey with God and they also become truths that we now have authority to share. This is the break-through moment for my students in the writing class.

One of my greatest joys is witnessing an artist spring to life with inspiration after one of our powerful devotionals. They are now no longer an artist searching for inspiration, but they have become the receiver of a weighty message and understand the importance of making it palatable to a new audience. When the gospel comes off the pages and into the hearts of my students, rapping becomes second nature. It suddenly becomes easy to rap, yet it is important to choose the right words. No longer will any ordinary word do the trick. With a message this great and important, they must find the most beautiful words to match this beautiful message. And this is the secret to being an amazing Christian rapper.

Teaching artists how to write has changed the way that I view talent. There is no such thing as a bad rapper to me anymore. There is only those who have not understood the beauty of what they are intending to communicate. Once an artist understands the beauty of the gospel, it is impossible to dilute it with mundane language. And there have been many times where I have enrolled an artist who most would consider terrible. These are artists who struggle with flow pattern, figurative language, and storytelling. But I always start at the same place. I do not dare attempt to challenge their flow, language, or story until I have first attempted to show them the beauty of Jesus. Because my artists are hand-selected and approved by me, this is rarely an introduction to Jesus. I generally only work with Christians because a person focused on communicating any other truth is not my target student. But I encourage them to engage with Jesus in a way that, most of the time, has been foreign or thought forbidden. We dive deep into their questions surrounding the texts, building up the main question that must be answered. And then we use the same text to insert Jesus as the answer to our deepest questions. What happens is always powerful. Electrifying, even! They see Jesus as beautiful and thus become determined to write it just as they see it in their mind.

In addition to my writing classes, my second plan was to create an artist development course. This class would focus solely on the heart posture of the artist. It would draw insight from my experiences in radio, label, and studio spaces. It would teach about the artists in the Bible and would study their approach to art and expression. I also wanted to highlight artists from the past and learn from them. I believe that history has much to teach the artist.

In these artist development classes, my students learn many of these truths that I have included in this book. They are encouraged to broaden their definition and understanding of an artist while also recognizing the subtleties that cause artists to fail. One in particular that we focus on is being an artist driven by self instead of by God. In an in-depth study that highlights the specific ways that God commissioned artists in the Bible, I teach strategies for how artists can endure for the long haul. Many of these classes touch on things such as integrity, worship, service, and humility.

I'm always inspired by the growth that happens with my students who take this class. It is a class that I highly recommend that they take *after* they have completed the writing sessions, but that order is not mandatory. These classes are where my students make some of the most important decisions about their careers, such as their artist name, brand, style, and purpose. I have the privilege of helping many artists determine, ahead of time, the ways in which they will not compromise. This is the class where money is emphasized as a tool and never as a goal. I clearly emphasize that financial success is not the metric a Christian artist is defined by. And once that has been understood, my artists are now empowered to actually make some real money.

In this class, I love being able to use great artists of history as blueprints, lessons, and warnings. Nothing is new under the sun, and encouraging artists to posture themselves to learn from anyone, no matter whether they are a believer or not, serves them well in their own journeys.

The remaining aspects that I teach in the artist development class are social media strategies and music business. No student's course is complete without ensuring that they understand the responsibility of stewarding their platforms well through social media and also understanding the journey of an independent artist. I teach all of my students about record labels, contracts, royalties, licensing, publishing, copyrights, and many of the other complicated aspects about the music business. My goal is not only to produce more artists that love Jesus and have amazing brands, but I am also intentionally making sure that Christian artists become smarter in business and increase in ownership.

These are empowering tools for the Christian artist and will prevent many artists from being taken advantage of by industry opportunists.

After my first two plans of writing classes and artist development, my third plan was to assist artists in the areas of PR and media relations. For this, I would use the skills that I had obtained during my time at Atlantic Records to highlight and bring exposure to artists that I strongly believe in. I would utilize my network, contacts, and writing skills to help ensure that the artists I work with are seen by as many people as possible. I would commit to exposing the artists that I believe are hidden gems of the culture.

For this portion of my services, artists hire my company for a minimum three-month PR contract. These services focus on taking a well-developed brand to the next level by connecting them with fans, curators, and other brands that mutually add value to each other. At the time, with an understanding of how rapid our culture consumes music, my focus was on connecting artists to strong digital platforms that yield streams, sales, and direct-to-consumer connections. Because my company's reputation becomes heavily intertwined with the artists that we represent, we are highly selective on who we work with for our limited PR services. I prefer to work with artists that have already completed my writing session and artist development courses. This generally assures me that the artist I am working hard to pitch understands their mission and is committed to it. Minor setbacks and rejections won't discourage these artists. They anticipate resistance due to the large mission they carry. These artists and their hunger also motivate me to make sure that I find the best placements as possible for them.

As fluid and concrete as my plan was, it took some time for me to have the courage to execute it. My first few months of offering these services came at no cost and simply flowed out of my desire to mentor young artists. During phone calls with my artist friends, I recognized the need for Biblical discipleship. I discovered that I am so passionate about artists having the correct heart posture that I didn't want to build any music careers apart from ensuring that the artists are first anchored in a relationship with Jesus. The music industry has many superstars but not many disciples. And that was my burden.

This desire to see artists flourish both in their faith and in their music met its trial run with the Row Men. Trubl3, BlessThePen, and I began meeting twice a week to study the Bible. Our friendship and everyday conversation had revealed that we all had gaps in our faith and theology that needed to be filled with intentional time spent in the Word. We decided it was best to place both of their music careers on a temporary halt as we sought to ensure that our faith was built on the solid rock of Christ. After three months of intense Bible study, I discovered that both Trubl3 and BlessThePen didn't fully grasp what Jesus had accomplished on the Cross. I recognized that deeply understanding the gospel was far more important than the music they desired to make. Their souls were on the line.

At this time, my passion for the Bible was extremely high. I was enrolled in a fast-track seminary course sponsored by the Fellowship of Christian Athletes (FCA) and was learning so much about the Bible, its historical context, and even the languages it was written in. I had a deeper undergirding of my faith and an understanding of the unique differences between all of Paul's letters. I recognized that many of Trubl3 and BlessThePen's theological gaps were addressed in the book of Romans and decided that we would take a slow journey through the entire book. We were going to study the book of Romans line by line and verse by verse.

Though the book of Romans is a relatively short book, the pace we were moving at was slow and intentional. It took us about two months to read the first three chapters! After we finally finished reading the third chapter, I decided to check in with the guys to see how they were being challenged and what they had received from our time studying this book. After realizing that both Trubl3 and BlessThePen were struggling to believe what they had read, I decided that it would be best for us to start completely over from the beginning. BlessThePen and Trubl3 were growing and were determined to be men who believed the Bible over what they saw with their physical eyes.

As we restarted Romans, I felt a breakthrough as the men committed to renew their minds and have faith in what the apostle Paul was declaring Jesus had accomplished. With our faith anchored in Jesus, I decided to incorporate writing challenges and prompts based off of what we were reading in Romans. I discovered that deeply processing the Bible cannot solely be internal but must be wrestled with, considered, and even brought into our own world and language.

Before we knew it, we were all understanding what we were reading on a deeper level as we processed it through our writing challenges. I had discovered that writing could also become a tool used in discipleship to ensure that artists are able to understand what they are reading in the Bible. I didn't realize it at the time, but the Lord was developing my style of discipleship. It was one that was focused on community and the complete authority of the Scriptures. It was committed to a faithful witness of Jesus and a life of confession and accountability. It was hip-hop at its core.

Eventually, Trubl3, BlessThePen, and I decided to compile our best writing from the book of Romans and to release it as a project. When it came time to brand ourselves and discover our name, we decided we would call ourselves the Row Men. We chose this name for obvious reasons due to the fact that our bond as Christian brothers and artists was strengthened by an in-depth Bible study of the book of Romans. Our album released on November 30, 2020 and was an instant success.

That initial process taught me a lot about how the Lord would continue to use me in the future. I now had clarity in the work that I was called to do outside of my own independent career. And my next task would be to rest, knowing that the Lord is able to sustain the faith of my mentees in seasons when I am no longer present.

Every person needs a mentor, and every person also needs a mentee. This balance is how we keep our legacy continuing and expanding. There are many people who have mentors, but sadly everything they are learning from their mentors ends with themselves. They have not committed to sharing the knowledge and helping others grow. And what usually happens is that people who are full of knowledge, without any habit of sharing it with others, usually drown in their own self-consumption. The truth is that we are able to hold more by giving more away. There are many leaders who have all of the skills and knowledge necessary to be successful yet continue to be frustrated with their own lack of progress and breakthrough. Much of this can be attributed to a lack of faith. If we believe that God does not have the power to bless more than one person at once, we will often become selfish and hoard knowledge that God has given us for the benefit and blessing of others.

Your neighbor's success does not equal your failure. This is a worldly belief that is far from true and that hurts entire communities and networks of people. Because God designed and created us all to be in community and fellowship with others, we must understand that our success is deeply interwoven with the flourishing of our neighbors. If I am successful, but everyone around me is struggling, then I am not actually successful. A man is not measured solely by the work of his hands but by the strength of his community. It takes a village to raise a child and a community to develop a well-rounded individual. A person cannot learn to love by themself. They must have someone to love, and therefore, a person on an island is doomed for destruction. I am not who I am simply because I come from a two-parent household. Many have come from two-parent households and never reached their full potential. I am who I am today because of the men and women who have taken me under their wings and mentored me. And through this, I've observed a funny thing: everybody wants to be a teacher, but nobody wants to be taught.

I have dedicated my life to being both a mentor and a mentee. I desire to be a lifelong learner, always acknowledging that my growth isn't complete as long as I'm alive on this earth. I am moving from glory to glory and becoming more like Jesus every day. And much of that growth happens when I seek to surround myself with people who are greater than myself. It is a humbling posture that I must increasingly grow in, yet the implications of it are extremely rewarding. All of us are a product of the five people we spend the most time with. These people either inspire us to challenge ourselves or they inflate our view of self and hinder growth. This is because we are rarely growing if we don't believe that we have more room to grow.

In a culture where many people see the impact of having a mentor, few see the positives associated with having a mentee. And for this reason, many Christian rappers and creatives have no anchor or bearing on their identity or even on their gifts and talents. Being both a mentor and mentee helps the Christian artist properly see themselves. Because they are a mentor, they walk in confidence, witnessing the value that they bring to the lives of others. And because they are a mentee, they are aware that they still have much to learn and to develop to maximize their impact.

Being a mentor doesn't have to be a formal inauguration. Sometimes, it is simply recognizing someone with a similar passion as you who isn't quite as developed. It is being intentional about investing in this individual with no expectation of a return other than to see them flourish and avoid the same mistakes that you made. These relationships hold

Christian creatives accountable because they have someone watching them and studying their life. A sense of responsibility becomes inevitable in the lives of Christians who have mentees. They are often more intentional in their private lives, which ultimately becomes displayed publicly at God's appointed time.

When I was a young artist in Atlanta, it was the older rappers from my church that mentored me. When I was in college, it was Allen Reynolds, Dr. Lindsey Warren, Reverend Bernard Richardson, and many others. In the music industry, it has been Sydney Margetson, Patricia, and Jason Davis. I have learned and grown from all of these people. And most often, the best mentors don't even realize they are creating a lifelong impact. They are generally just being themselves.

One of the things I love about the mentor-mentee dynamic is that sometimes the roles change. In almost every circumstance where I have been a mentor, I have ended up learning and being developed by my mentee. It is one of the amazing things that happens when you commit to doing life with others and when you remind yourself to remain humble. On the days where I am most confident in what I know or have experienced, it is particularly important for me to remember that my mentee has much to teach me. Because all humans are made in the image of God, each person has value and therefore should have value to me. We must fight to see people the way God sees them, desperately seeking where they can reveal more of God to us.

If Jesus was a rapper, He would be both a mentor and a mentee. In Luke 2, the Bible tells us that Jesus was found in the temple, sitting among the teachers, listening to them and asking them questions. Wow! Do you see how powerful this is? That God himself chose to learn from men whom He created! If this doesn't inspire a generation to seek mentorship, then I don't know what else will. And then, later, Jesus had the twelve disciples, which I'll equate to a sort of mentor-mentee relationship.

CHAPTER 12 SOW AND TELL

And because Jesus was the humblest man that ever lived, He probably learned many things from His disciples as well. And then to put a bow on top of all of this, His disciples and apostles went on to continue the model that Jesus had set for them. The most famous example that we all know of is Paul, who went on to mentor Timothy later in his ministry.

I believe that it is important for Christian creatives to restore value to the mentor-mentee relationship. A quote that my dad always said when I was growing up is "People are our greatest asset." I believe this is true and that this is also biblical. God has given us a tremendous gift in community. There are lessons, blessings, and wisdom that God has intentionally deposited in the lives of our neighbors. Many Christians have spent years in isolation, praying for something that God wants to give them through another person. How can we claim to be like Jesus by ourselves when He himself was rooted in community? Jay-Z mentored Kanye West and Kanye West mentored Travis Scott. Who are your mentors, and who are your mentees?

CHAPTER 13

LEGACY

One of the most important lessons that I've embraced is understanding the rise and fall of leaders. In this chapter, I'm not
speaking about leaders falling from grace or falling into miscon-
duct. Instead, I'm speaking about leaders intentionally falling from
the top spot so that others can have the opportunity to lead. God has
designed the natural trajectory of life with plenty of space for all of us
to hit our peaks within our prospective callings and areas of expertise.
No one is created to lead forever. The only reign that is eternal belongs
to Christ. We all have been allotted a portion of time in which we are
to steward our roles and influence to bring God glory. Understanding
this motivates us to maximize the short time we have in the spotlight
so that we can ultimately point people to the light that shines forever –
Jesus. My goal as a rapper has never been to rap forever, nor should it
be. My goal is to faithfully steward my rap platform with integrity and
excellence as long as the Spirit leads me to rap.

I look to the day when I am no longer in the spotlight with great antic-
ipation. And the parts of myself that desire to choose sadness must
understand that they are the lesser influence. It is okay to be sad for
when that day shall come, but it is more of a celebration than mourning.

If I have faithfully lived out my calling within the field of hip-hop, then I will have much to celebrate on that day. And the steps that I have taken today are part of me cementing that work. At the writing of this book, I am still very much in love with hip-hop and the exercise of using words to communicate the gospel in code. I get a rush of energy just by thinking about creating a new song and still know I have much to improve on in my writing. I am still an underdog and still have many people that do not see anything great about my music or what I have created. And this is a beautiful thing because in hip-hop, once an artist is highly respected, they often lose their grit. They no longer rap with desperation. They are immune to the pangs of hunger and their dreams are different.

I've never had a number one album, and I've never even landed on Billboard. Most people in the mainstream have never heard of me, yet I still believe in the vision God gave me as a child: that my music would touch the world and usher in revival in the music industry. It will no longer be acceptable to create music that is poisoning faith and the soul. The best rappers will be those who are not just living for this world but who are anticipating the world that is to come. I believe this is my calling.

My albums were written living check-to-check, lacking a future, and on an "oatmeal for breakfast, lunch, and dinner" diet. If I'm no longer writing with that same desperation, then it's time for me to leave the game and make way for someone else who is hungry. The very presence I lacked in my career is who I have vowed to be for someone else. I always desired a rap mentor and have even been laughed at for publicly vocalizing that. It's long understood as something uncommon and unnatural in hip-hop. But I've realized how that thinking has held us back for so long. Imagine if I had a rap mentor in 2014. Imagine if I had someone who challenged me to write rap the way that I challenge my artists. And this is why I'm filling that gap.

The album I'm working on now has never been done before. There's nothing new under the sun, but there have been many revolutions since God sent a soldier to create an album like this. And I'm grateful that God has filled me with inspiration to do what I love at the level that I'm able to do it. The sticky note sitting on my board in front of me says that I'm believing that this book will be a New York Times Bestseller. My publisher probably wouldn't want me to include this sentence, but I believe in writing the vision down. Hopefully, this work goes on to inspire many other artists and Christians to give their creative selves fully to God. I used to feel like a lot of my work was not being heard, but I continued to be obedient and do the music that I knew God was telling me to do. It's amazing to hear that people have been discovering me and going back into my catalog.

My journey has been a lot of determination. Since I've moved to New York, I've been learning how to navigate all the different nuances of what it means to be an artist in a saturated market. Everybody is a rapper, and it's become very trendy to be a rapper. I've had to find ways to separate myself and figure out how to stay relevant since I began creating music at eight years old. It is the balance of finding something new while staying rooted in my sound and identity.

In this new season of being married, I finally feel like an adult. For some reason, most of my life I've always considered myself a teenager. I've now been in a space where I'm newly married, and it's prompting a lot of changes in my expression.

I'm technically not a young artist anymore, but I'm not an old artist either. I consider myself as sitting right in the middle of two hip-hop generations. I'm not a hip-hop founder, but I'm also not in this new style of hip-hop. This allows me to connect to the pioneers of hip-hop and the genre while still having a deep appreciation for the new artists that are emerging today. I've learned how to appreciate all expressions of hip-hop because the genre itself is only a reflection of the world the artists live in. I don't think it's fair for us to expect a whole generation that is living a completely different life than Nas to create the music that Nas created. This is why I feel like judging hip-hop by anything other than the art form isn't completely fair. Styles and content will change. The way that it moves your soul remains the same.

My biggest critique of Christians is that they love with the wrong motive. It's often...they only love you so that you will believe in their God. But this is not how it works. We have to love people so intentionally and so honestly and so real that if they never believe and never change, our love doesn't change. If we loved people with the commitment that "I'ma do life with you, be here by your side whether I agree with you or not," we'd see the world change. But instead, we're not committed to that process, and we think we're going to get on stage and spit a verse, and then everybody is going to get saved. We oftentimes miss out on rejoicing and celebrating the many steps it takes to get somebody to salvation. God is always reminding me how much He loves people. And how much He's willing to do whatever it takes to make sure that they are saved. How much He pursues us, even though we are constantly running from Him. How much He doesn't hold our past mistakes against us. And this is the message that keeps me going. It's these times where He reminds me that His greatness is revealed by my greatness. I've committed to sticking to the process. And no one can tell me that the people I've met so far on my journey weren't worth it.

I've accomplished the things that I have because of an unwavering awareness of God's presence in my life. On most days, I'm constantly reminding myself that God is with me, and I've learned that simple awareness of His presence makes much of the difference in my life. In 2017, I performed a hundred and twenty shows. I had made it my goal to do at least one performance every three days. I had no opportunities for touring at the time, and nobody was offering me money to perform.

I had recently been featured in *Complex Magazine* and was working on my album *We Are & We Shall*. The Lord was stirring my heart more than ever, and I was seeing the impact of my performances on the crowds. Many times when I left the stage, people would pull me to the side asking me to pray for them or they would share with me about how they heard God's voice while I was performing. These were the moments that fueled me to keep going. Knowing that Jesus was using me to reach people outside of the church was special.

Discipline and strict scheduling were how I managed to perform those one hundred and twenty shows. Every Sunday after church, I would log on to Eventbrite searching for performance opportunities. I used the keywords "open mic" and "showcase" to find performances. I restricted my search locations to Atlanta, the DMV, New York, and Chicago. Performing in these cities allowed me to build hometown fanbases in places where I wouldn't have to pay for a hotel. Because these shows weren't paid opportunities, I made sure to get a bulk of CDs printed so that I could sell them at my performances. Every Sunday, I would schedule three performances for the upcoming week. Due to many open mics operating on a first come, first served basis, I would always make sure I contacted the hosts ahead of time to secure a performance slot so that my traveling wouldn't be in vain. This also allowed me to reach out to my network and alert people about where I would be performing that week.

For travel, I couldn't afford flights, so I took buses to get around. My friends knew me as being the bus king! I would take thirty to fifty-dollar buses for sixteen to twenty hours just to arrive at the scheduled city to perform. I knew that meant I only needed to sell six to ten CDs to break even on my travel expenses. It wasn't the most comfortable or glamorous way to travel, but outside of my circle of friends, the world never knew how I was getting around. Every time they looked up, I was in another city performing, but they didn't know it had taken me a full day to get there on the bus. Yet I was having a kingdom impact in the cities that I loved and felt called to. It was a beautiful time.

I highlight this season in my career to show you that the road to reaching the masses is not easy. It is very difficult and will require many sacrifices. And just as I was quiet about my traveling methods back then, I want to remain that way whether I am still taking the bus or catching a flight. Doing whatever is necessary to serve the people is the route I'm going to take.

I've already determined that I could be wrong about everything that I've written in this book as well as everything that I've said in my music. But my daily prayer is, "Lord, if I'm wrong, let me not hinder your work." I'm going to take a million risks in front of the eyes of the whole world, and no matter if it's uncomfortable at times, I hope they know they can stick with me through the journey and know that I'm a man of my word. That I started this thing with God, and I'm going to finish it with Him.

If the world never knows me by my music, by my heart, by my style, they will know me as somebody who called forth greatness out of people. I hate that the world has lied to people and told them that it's wrong to want to be great. Being humble is knowing you're nothing without God. The first step to becoming great is to stop caring about becoming great. I'm only here to be perfectly who He created me to be.

Regardless of the rules that you feel govern your art form or restrict how you want to express yourself, do what's in your heart. Ultimately, you'll only regret doing something that's not true to you, but if you do what's in your heart, there's never a feeling that you sold out or like you didn't do what you should've done.

One of the things I've recently given much of my time to is investing in new artists. I believe that Jesus left us with a model of discipleship and a method of growth that is based on multiplication. He reached twelve, that reached some, that eventually compounded into a global message of faith. As an artist for over twenty years, I've finally realized that my success in the music industry cannot be based on my career alone. It should be reflected in how many other artists I inspire who use their talents and gifts for God. I believe the Lord has given me a mantle of authority in the sphere of music and entertainment. So, how can I not help ensure that there will be other artists who are also committed to sharing the message of Jesus?

One of the reasons people don't follow Jesus is because Christians have made all these rules and prerequisites that Jesus himself has not even made. Jesus comes to us with a simple statement. And that statement is "Follow me." He doesn't tell us where we're going or what the journey will be like. Yet the statement remains the same. It's going to command a lot of trust and faith in Him as our shepherd to follow Him blindly, especially when the road isn't paved.

I want to be remembered as an artist who removed the barriers and obstacles that keep people from Jesus. These barriers are man-made, religious, and demonic. And they ultimately keep us in bondage as we struggle to please God in our strength. I desire that anyone who comes into contact with me, personally or through any art form that I have created, feels the freedom and ease of coming to Jesus. I am no longer seeking to push them into His arms. Early in my career, that was my mission. But now, I've realized that even believing that I have the power to do that is pride and arrogance. It is truly the Spirit that opens our eyes and allows us to recognize that we need God. And He does it in His timing, in conjunction with us acknowledging our weakness and lack of power. Recognizing this has removed a tremendous amount of pressure and has freed me to create art from an offensive posture instead of a defensive one.

Too many Christian artists create as if we are losing the battle against culture. I choose to create as if we are winning. I've seen different effects simply from shifting my perspective. When I created music that pushed people into a lifestyle that they weren't looking for, I only worked against the gospel. These hearers often became even more hard-hearted against the gospel than they were initially. I had to face the fact that I was pushing them further away.

And part of my success in making the shift was gaining my understanding of the gospel in my life. It also required me to humble myself and confess an even greater need for God. When I remembered how I came to Jesus, a lightbulb turned on in my head. I didn't come to Jesus because the pastor told me it was the right choice to make. Pastor Green never communicated that. Instead, he shared with the church about how nothing would ever stop Jesus from loving us. And how every day, for the rest of our life, He would always be there, patiently waiting for us to decide to trust Him. This is the day my feet shifted and felt glued to the floor.

When Pastor Green did the altar call, he felt no pressure to fill the altar all at once. All he felt was the pressure to share about how available God's love was at that moment. When I realized that today, tomorrow, and even as far as my five-year-old brain could think ahead, that Jesus would still be waiting on me to trust Him, I realized that I didn't want to wait any longer. And this is precisely how we win the world.

When I get on stage, I look into the crowd and fight to remind myself that God loves every single person in the audience. And that the enemy has been telling them all their lives that they have to clean themselves up first before Jesus will accept them. And then once I recognize the lie that is widely believed, I commit to not leaving that stage or platform without telling the truth. Jesus loves all of them *now!* He always has and He always will. And realizing that there is a harvest waiting, I proceed to do what Jesus would do if He was a rapper.

ABOUT THE AUTHOR

Cellus Hamilton is a hip-hop artist based in NYC. Since the age of eight years old, he has shifted the culture. Raised in Atlanta, the young artist was influenced by his mother, who was a buzzing hip-hop artist. As a well-traveled musician and an alumnus of Howard University, Hamilton's education and exposure to different regions have established him as a dynamic voice of faith within the hip-hop community. Cellus Hamilton also has a background in seminary and has worked with the Fellowship of Christian Athletes.

As a frequent performer, Cellus Hamilton also can be found speaking in prisons, sports camps, and business summits. He is an electric performer known for his stage presence energy. Hamilton is also notably passionate about family and marriage, as he is a podcast host alongside his wife. Cellus Hamilton currently resides in Harlem, New York with his wife Denya and his son Simeon.

Made in the USA
Middletown, DE
22 June 2023